# REVOLUTIONARY RECORDS

OF

# MARYLAND

By

GAIUS MARCUS BRUMBAUGH

AND

MARGARET ROBERTS HODGES

CLEARFIELD

Reprinted for
Clearfield Company, Inc. by
Genealogical Publishing Co., Inc.
Baltimore, Maryland
1991, 1996, 1999, 2003


Originally published: Washington, D.C., 1924
Reprinted: Genealogical Publishing Co., Inc.
Baltimore, 1967, 1978
Library of Congress Catalogue Card Number 67-28608
International Standard Book Number 0-8063-0061-2
*Made in the United States of America*

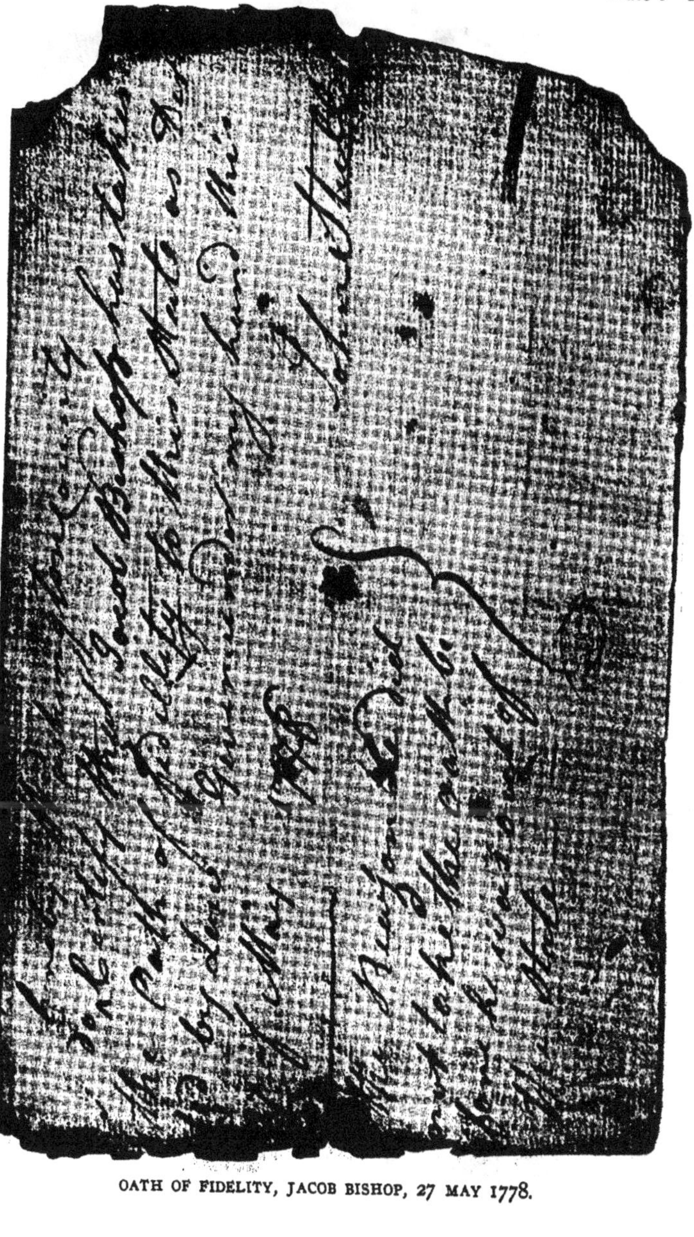

Plate I—III

OATH OF FIDELITY, JACOB BISHOP, 27 MAY 1778.

OATH OF FIDELITY, JACOB BISHOP (REVERSE)

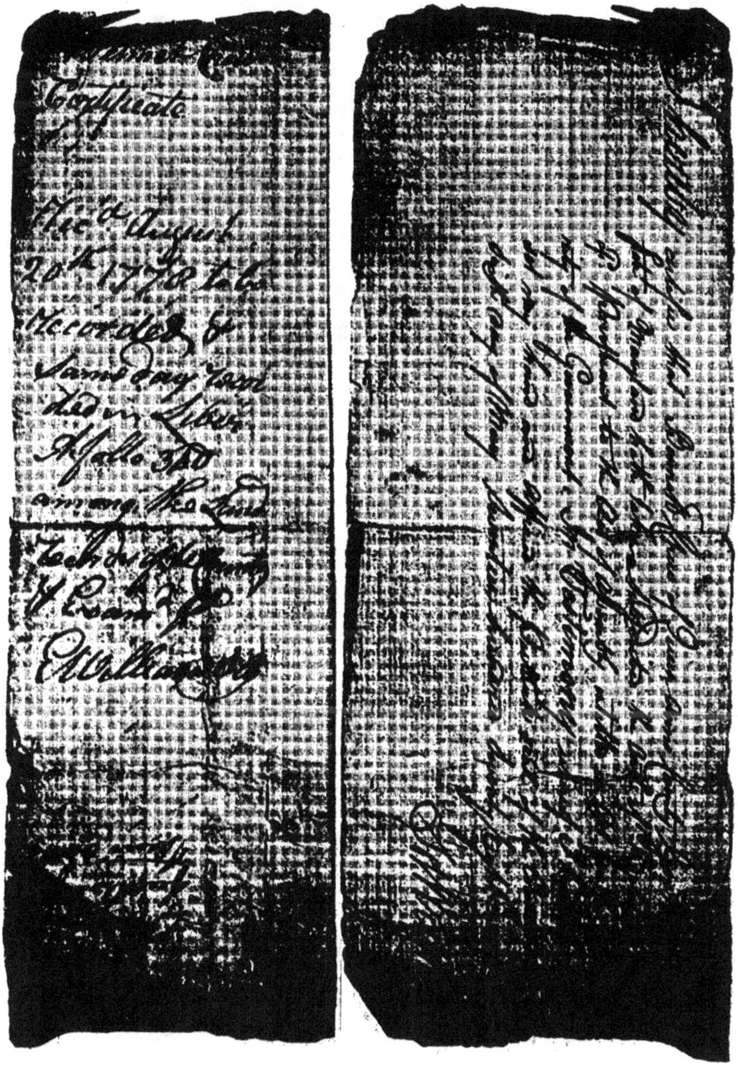

OATH OF FIDELITY, BENNETT CHEW, 6 MAY 1778

OATH OF FIDELITY, EDWARD TILGHMAN, 6 MAY 1778.

# PREFACE

Mrs. Margaret Roberts Hodges (Mrs. George W.) discovered in various places in Maryland important records covering the Colonial and Revolutionary periods in American history. She transcribed much of the same and presented a valuable series of Maryland Revolutionary manuscript volumes to the Library of the National Society, Daughters of the American Revolution. The proper officers of the latter organization, the Maryland Historical Society, and also patriotic individuals have very kindly and fully assisted the plan to publish such materials by placing at our disposal numerous important unpublished records of Maryland. Amongst these individuals Mr. Caleb Clarke Magruder, Jr., deserves especial thanks for furnishing the records and abstracts herein published upon pages 25 to 36. The latter are hitherto unknown and inaccessible records of civil services, and are of special value in supporting applications for membership in the various patriotic societies. The entire contents of Part One are valuable for this purpose.

Invaluable early Maryland records may be in the hands of librarians and individuals throughout the Nation, and extensive benefit may result from having such brought to the attention of the undersigned for inclusion in the plan to make some of such records more generally accessible.

The selected records are to be published in a series of pamphlets, as the subscriptions may justify, in limited edition and each pamphlet containing a *full index*. Part One is herewith offered to all who are interested in Maryland history, and subscriptions will be entered for the proposed series. There is a close relation between this series and the materials contained in *"Maryland Records—Brumbaugh,"* of which Vol. I was published in 1915.

The Act of Assembly, 5 February, 1777, required that the Oath of Fidelity and Support be taken by all citizens, especially all holding positions of trust, all voting at any election, all transacting business in Maryland; and even citizens of one county who transacted business in another county were required to record their Oath in the latter county—see Plates I-IV. The "Test Oath," or "Oath of Fidelity and Support," was most important in Revolutionary times, and could not be lightly taken.

In February Session, 1777, No. 1, we find:

*Resolved,* That Messrs. Thomas Brooke Hodgkin, Wm. Wilkins and John Johnson,—be appointed a board of auditors[a]—by taking the oath of fidelity to this state, and an oath well, diligently and faithfully to execute the duty of their office agreeable to this resolve and by subscribing their belief in the Christian religion, etc.

Jan. 21, 1778[b]—"The Committee appointed to devise effectual means to prevent persons disaffected to the interests of the United States from being employed in any of the important offices thereof, beg leave to report the following Resolutions:" etc.

---

[a] Auditors for all State accounts, the late Conventions, Councils of Safety, Gen. Assembly, Governor, etc.

[b] Journ., Cont. Cong., Vol. 10. p. 68.

Feb. 3, 1778,[c] The Congress passed the resolution based upon the foregoing report:

*Resolved,* That every officer who holds or shall hereafter hold a commission or office from Congress, shall take and subscribe the following oath or affirmation:

I, ————, do acknowledge the United States of America to be free, independent and sovereign states, and declare that the people thereof owe no allegiance or obedience to George the Third, King of Great Britain; and I renounce, refuse and abjure any allegience or obedience to him; and I do swear (or affirm) that I will, to the utmost of my power, support, maintain and defend the said United States against the said King George the Third and his heirs and successors, and his and their abettors, assistants and adherents, and will serve the United States in the office of ———— which I now hold, with fidelity according to the best of my skill and understanding. So help me God.[d]

The various states were also directed to take similar action, immediately. The resolutions passed 21 Oct., 1776, prescribing the form of an oath or affirmation were also repealed.

*Gaius Marcus Brumbaugh*

Washington, D. C., May 7, 1924.

c Same, p. 114.

d On the adoption of this resolution Messrs. Forbes and Henry, Md. delegates voted "no"—the only such votes.

# REVOLUTIONARY RECORDS
## OF
# MARYLAND *

## MONTGOMERY COUNTY, MARYLAND, MARCH COURT, 1778.

'A LIST OF PERSONS IN MONTGOMERY COUNTY WHO HAVE TAKEN THE FOLLOW-
ING OATH BEFORE THE DIFFERENT MAGISTRATES AS MENTIONED
BELOW; AND RETURNED BY THEM TO MONTGOMERY COURT."
"OATH OF FIDELITY AND SUPPORT."

"I do sware I do not hold myself bound to yield any Allegience or obedience to the King of Great Britain his heirs or Successors and that I will be true
and faithful to the State of Maryland and will to the utmost of my power, Support maintain and defend the Freedom and Independence thereof and the Government as now established against all open enemies and secret and traterous
Conspriaces and will use my utmost endeavours to disclose and make known
to the Governor or some one of the Judges or Justices thereof all Treasons or
Treaterous Consperaces, attempts or Combinations against this State or the
Government thereof which may come to my Knowledge so help me God.
Taken before the Worshipfull

GERRARD BRISCOE.

Eleven Returns, 1598 men. A true copy from a copy of the original,
Maryland Historical Society—surnames placed first for convenience of reference.

------

* Pages 1-24 were published in the April and July, 1917, (Vol. VI, Nos. 1,2) issues of
the National Genealogical Society Quarterly to call special attention to this proposed volume. (Pp. 21, 22 contain additional extracts from Kilty's Laws.)

Signatures thus marked (*) are   x   in original record.
mark
his

## 1 The Worshipfull Gerrard Briscoe's Returns.

| | | | | | |
|---|---|---|---|---|---|
| 2 | Burton, William, Sr. | 52 | Dougherty, Philip | 102 | Jarvis, Zadock |
| 3 | Burton, William, Jr. | 53 | Teeple, Isaac | 103 | Pack, Richard |
| 4 | Montgomery, William | 54 | Malone, Thomas | 104 | Selby, Thomas, Sr. |
| 5 | Gordon, Joseph | 55 | Suter, John | 105 | Welling, John |
| 6 | Speak, Nicholas | 56 | Collins, Edward | 106 | Ricketts, Anthony |
| 7 | Longland, Thomas | 57 | Cobert, Aaron | 107 | Jarvis, Elisha |
| 8 | Holt, Thomas | 58 | Speak, William | 108 | Selby, Zachariah |
| 9 | Ray, John, Jr. | 59 | Fryer, Richard | 109 | Sansberry, William |
| 10 | Gaither, Basil | 60 | Sheppan, Thomas | 110 | Selby, Richard |
| 11 | Birdwhistle, Thomas | 61 | Heater, George | 111 | Mullikin, Lewis, Sr. |
| 12 | Seager, John | 62 | House, William | 112 | Sibert, Henry |
| 13 | Pinchback, John | 63 | Pack, Thomas | 113 | Goolden, Samuel |
| 14 | Belt, John | 64 | Yost, Tobias | 114 | Davis, Griffith |
| 15 | Simpson, James | 65 | Edwards, John Bridget | 115 | Eads, Saml. |
| 16 | Waters, Isaac | 66 | Ezekiah, Roberts | 116 | Hilleary, John |
| 17 | Waters, Nancy | 67 | Bruce, John | 117 | Hilleary, Henry |
| 18 | Dobbs, Thomas | 68 | Dougherty, Neal | 118 | Holland, Benjamin, Jr |
| 19 | Higdon, Benjamin | 69 | Holland, Archibald | 119 | Davis, Richard |
| 20 | Tracy, William | 70 | Leach, William, Jr. | 120 | Holland, Abraham |
| 21 | Williams, Benjamin | 71 | Fields, Abraham | 121 | Heathman, George |
| 22 | Darby, Josiah | 72 | Leach, Thomas | 122 | Riley, Zachariah |
| 23 | Pack, William, Sr. | 73 | Leach, John | 123 | Trail, Archibald |
| 24 | Trail, David, Jr. | 74 | Crysp, Friday | 124 | Hardesty, Samuel |
| 25 | McBee, Allen | 75 | Adamson, Basil | 125 | Gittings, Henry |
| 26 | Hawker, Philip | 76 | Davis, Charles (of Griffith) | 126 | Burdett, Benjamin |
| 27 | Trail, Basil | 77 | Adamson, John | 127 | Greenberry, Gaither |
| 28 | O'Neal, Charles | 78 | Waters, Zachariah | 128 | Fields, Mathew |
| 29 | Saffel, William | 79 | Waters, William | 129 | Gaither, Nicholas |
| 30 | Lynn, John | 80 | Case, Thomas | 130 | Wilson, John |
| 31 | Anderson, James | 81 | Athins, William | 131 | Wheat, Joseph |
| 32 | Read, Thomas (Clk.) | 82 | Selby, Thomas, Jr. | 132 | Wheat, Azariah |
| 33 | Davis, Lodowick | 83 | Trail, James, Sr. | 133 | Bruce, Charles |
| 34 | Riley, James | 84 | Kelly Benjamin | 134 | Wheat, John |
| 35 | Bernard, Jacob | 85 | Leach, William, Sr. | 135 | Ennis, Nicholas |
| 36 | Smith, Vachel | 86 | Sheckell, Abraham | 136 | Case, James |
| 37 | Heathman, John | 87 | Buxton, William | 137 | Hawker, William |
| 38 | Ducker, Nathanel | 88 | Trail, William | 138 | Dougherty, John |
| 39 | Leg, Thomas | 89 | Benson, William | 139 | McBee, Ninian |
| 40 | Riley, Jeremiah | 90 | Nichols, Thomas | 140 | Yost, Lodowick |
| 41 | Rawlings, John | 91 | Mullekin, Lewis | 141 | Brnond, Burdit Gray |
| 42 | Smith, John | 92 | Cath, John | 142 | Briscoe, Robert |
| 43 | Buxton, John | 93 | Cash, William | 143 | West, Joseph |
| 44 | Seybert, George | 94 | Carey, James | 144 | West, Thomas |
| 45 | Saffel, Charles | 95 | Cahill, Dennis | 145 | Case, Brock |
| 46 | Candler, Daniel | 96 | Cash, Dawson | 146 | Harriss, Nathaniel |
| 47 | Trail, David, Sr. | 97 | Cash, John | 147 | Leach, Benjamin |
| 48 | Kelly, Thomas | 98 | Allison, Pacey | 148 | Leach, Josiah |
| 49 | McDermett, Patrick | 99 | Derham, Patrick | 149 | Chattle, Thomas |
| 50 | McDavit, John | 100 | Trott, Henry | 150 | Bathe, Theophilus |
| 51 | Stanby, Michael | 101 | Taylor, James | 151 | Betts, Higginson |

MONTGOMERY COUNTY, 2d March, 1778.

May it please your Excellency and the Right Honerable the Counsel.
The above is a true Transcript from my Book which Contains the Oath and Affirmation of Fidelity, and the names of those that have taken Repeated and Subscribed the Oath and Affirmation of Fidelity and Support to the State of Maryland. I am Gentlemen

Your most Obedant Humble Servant,

GERD BRISCOE.

To His Excellency Thos. Johnson, Esq., Governor and to The Right Honorable the Council of Maryland.

## 1 *The Worshipfull Edward Burgess' Returns.*

| | | |
|---|---|---|
| 2 Williams, Charles | 73 Mullikin, Basil | 142 Walters, Weavour |
| 3 Lacklen, John | 74 Barnes, Richard Weavour | 143 Snell, George |
| 4 Lansdale, Thos. Lancaster | 75 Hiland, Hugh | 144 Roby, Berry |
| 5 Beggezley, Benjamin | 76 Griffith, Benjamin | 145 Lazenby, Henry |
| 6 Byan, William | 77 Pigman, Nathaniel | 146 Harding, Charles |
| 7 Beall, Zephaniah | 78 Johnson, Thomas* | 147 Harding, Elias |
| 8 Beall, John | 79 Leck, Joseph | 148 Swearingen, Samuel |
| 9 Selby, Samuel | 80 Moore, John Williams | 149 Williams, William Prather |
| 10 Sheckell, John | 81 Lanum, Richard, Feb. 7th | 150 Willcoxen, John |
| 11 Lazenby, Alexander | 82 Hoskinson, Elisha | 151 Tannihill, John |
| 12 Fitzgarreld, William* | 83 Arme, Jeremiah | 152 Cashell, George |
| 13 Beall, Jeremiah* | 84 Brashears, Morris | 153 Garrott, Edward |
| 14 Meezes, Valentine | 85 Moore, Samuel | 154 Nittcoxen, Anthony |
| 15 Hocker, Nicholas | 86 Brashears, Morris, Jr. | 155 Shaw, William |
| 16 Jean, Zachariah Z.* | 87 Gartrell, Charles | 156 Willcoxen, George |
| 17 Rickets, Merchant* | 88 Bateman, John | 157 Willcoxen, John |
| 18 Beall, Robert | 89 Lucas, Basil | 158 Glaze, Samuel |
| 19 Beall, Jeremiah | 90 Reynolds, Charles | 159 Harding, John |
| 20 Gastrell, Francis | 91 Mitchell, Thomas* | 160 Harding, Edward |
| 21 Gastrell, John | 92 Litzgarreld, John* | 161 Harding, John |
| 22 Godman, Samuel Israel | 93 Wellmore, Robert | 162 Harding Josiah |
| 23 Mizers, Valentine | 94 Lewis, Daniel, Jr.* | 163 Beall, James (of James) |
| 24 Ducker, Jeremiah | 95 Case, Shadrach | 164 Beall, Alexander Edmonston |
| 25 Williams, Clement | 96 Linthycum, Archibald | |
| 26 Hall, Joseph, Jan 29, 1778 | 97 Culver, Henry | 165 Beall, Robert Asa |
| 27 Duke, William* | 98 Knott, Thomas | 166 Lewis, David |
| 28 Fitzgerrell, Richard* | 99 Lewis, Jeremiah | 167 Keen, James |
| 29 Berry, Nicholas | 100 Wheeler, Edward | 168 Shaw, James |
| 30 Beall, Ninian Edmonston | 101 Beall, Walter | 169 Odonald, Michael* |
| 31 White, Samuel Beall | 102 Fitzgarreld, Edward* | 170 Newsteep, Robert* |
| 32 Owen Robert | 103 Fitzgerrel, Mathew | 171 Beall, Daniel |
| 33 Lock, Henry, Sr. | 104 Beall, Joseph* | 172 Harding, William |
| 34 Kennedy, John | 105 Moore, Silvanus | 173 Beall, Zephaniah |
| 35 Berry, Richard | 106 Jones, Richard | 174 Perry, Erasmus |
| 36 Baker, John | 107 Davis, Henry Culver | 175 Dunn, Hugh Smith |
| 37 Bateson, William* | 108 Culver, Thomas | 176 Beall, Archibald |
| 38 Ridgeway, William | 109 Poch, Phillip | 177 Lackland, James |
| 39 Jarbeo, Gerard | 110 Tucker, John | 178 Harding, Basil |
| 40 Gartrell, Rich* | 111 Tucker, David | 179 Ferrell, John |
| 41 Gartrell, Joseph | 112 Beall, Robert | 180 Gates, Edward* |
| 42 Forset, James* | 113 Beall, Menum* | 181 Ferrell, James* |
| 43 Ruglass, James* | 114 Beall, David | 182 Glaze, Nathaniel |
| 44 Ridgerway, Masum | 115 Perry, Joseph | 183 Easten, John |
| 45 Jarboe, Henry Barton | 116 Galther, John | 184 Bigg, John |
| 46 Doran, Edward* | 117 Doaik, William | 185 Sellings, Hichard* |
| 47 Lanom, William* | 118 Berry, John | 186 Lacklin, Zadok |
| 48 Lewis, Daniel* | 119 Berry Jeremiah | 187 Hoskinson, Elisha |
| 49 Mitchel, Morrice* | 120 Owen, Thomas | 188 Macdougie, John |
| 50 Pigman, Mathew, Feb. 3rd | 121 Lazenby, Robert | 189 Macdougie, Samuel* |
| 51 Green, Ignatius | 122 Owen, John, Feb. 12th | 190 Peen, Benjamin* |
| 52 Owen, Capt. Robert | 123 Duvall, Lewis | 191 Mason, Jonthan |
| 53 Johnson, Thomas* | 124 Farmer, William | 192 Capell, Holland |
| 54 Gaither, Henry | 125 Owen, John Jr. | 193 Wesley, Humphrey* |
| 55 Nicholson, Joseph | 126 Owen, William | 194 Gartrell, Aaron* |
| 56 Johnson, John | 127 Quordren, John | 195 Swain, Robert |
| 57 Plummer, Philliman | 128 Peen, Benjamin | 196 Butt, Swerzinge* |
| 58 Mackelfresh, David | 129 Smith, Thomas* | 197 Butt, Samuel |
| 59 Mackelfresh, Richard | 130 Aldridge, Thomas | 198 Halland, William* |
| 60 Gue, Henry | 131 Mockabey, Brock* | 199 Holland, Nathan |
| 61 Mackelfresh, John* | 132 Nellson, Henry* | 200 Moore, Thomas |
| 62 Riggs, Samuel | 133 Murgrove, Samuel (son of Samuel) | 201 Dickerton, Serratt |
| 63 Chambers, Edwards | | 202 Rickket, Richard* |
| 64 Gaither, William | 134 Cullom, George | 203 Gaither, Ephraim |
| 65 Hallan, Joseph | 135 Peen, Edward | 204 Isade, Lazarus |
| 66 Reyos, John | 136 Applepe, Thomas | 205 Blowers, Benjamin |
| 67 Nicholson, William | 137 Perry, James* | 206 Chambers, John |
| 68 Mackelfresh, Richard* | 138 Musgrove, Samuel (son of Anthony) | 207 Sullivan, Cornelious |
| 69 Green, Richard | | 208 Borreman, George* |
| 70 Musgrove, John* | 139 Page, Jossey* | 209 Chambers, Josiah* |
| 71 Musgrove, Nathan | 140 Peen, Benjamin Davis | |
| 72 Gue, Joseph* | 141 Junnan, William | |

| 419 | Russell, Henry | 439 | Bryan, Richard | 459 | King, Edward |
|---|---|---|---|---|---|
| 420 | Ritchinson, William | 440 | Hurdle, Richard | 460 | McAtee, James |
| 421 | Richards, John | 441 | Ricketts, Benjamin, Sr. | 461 | Wyndham, William |
| 422 | Locker, Joseph | 442 | Perry, Joshua | 462 | Wellman, Bennett |
| 423 | Jewell, William | 443 | Mummart, John | 463 | Carrico, Thomas Ignatius |
| 424 | Perry, John | 444 | Constable, Robert | 464 | Oneale, David |
| 425 | Hurry, David | 445 | Cheney, Richard | 465 | Pelly, Harrison |
| 426 | Gray, Adin | 446 | Wilcoxen, Josiah | 466 | Mullikin, John |
| 427 | Baxter, Gabriel | 447 | Hooker, John | 467 | Thomas, Samuel, 3d, Jan. |
| 428 | Hill, John | 448 | Nixon, Jonathan | | 24. |
| 429 | Robinson, Leonard | 449 | Nixon, Richard | 468 | Cowmans, Richard |
| 430 | Bolsom, Thomas | 450 | Cullum, Francis | 469 | Brooke, James |
| 431 | Burton, Basil | 451 | Trail, James | 470 | Brooke, Roger |
| 432 | Smallwood, William | 452 | Offutt, Nathan | 471 | Brooke, Thomas |
| 433 | Browning, Joseph | 453 | Darnall, Isaac | 472 | Robertson, George |
| 434 | Balled, Richard | 454 | Steel, William | 473 | Brooke, Samuel |
| 435 | King, John | 455 | Steel, John | 474 | Walters, Thomas |
| 436 | Ballard, John | 456 | Steel, James | 475 | Ward, Joseph, Mch. 10, '78 |
| 437 | Collins, Nathan | 457 | McCrae, Zephaman | 476 | Thomas, Richard, Jr., |
| 438 | Collins, John | 458 | Summers, Benjamin | | Mch. 10, '78. |

475 and 476 "Affirmed before the Court." True Copy from the original Book Ledger in Montgomery County Court by

EDW. BURGESS.

1 *The Worshipfull Joseph Wilson's Returns, Jan. 19th, 1778.*

| 2 | Nicholls, John Hayman | 40 | Low, David | 79 | Medley, William |
|---|---|---|---|---|---|
| 3 | Nicholls, Thomas | 41 | Baily, John* | 80 | Farmer, John* |
| 4 | Jordon, James | 42 | Lilley, William* | 81 | Smith, Basil |
| 5 | Peack, Thomas | 43 | Offutt, Zackh. | 82 | Dawson, John* |
| 6 | Oneill, Henry | 44 | Gaither, Burgess | 83 | Roberts, Basil |
| 7 | Harding, Clement | 45 | Chesher, John Nicholls | 84 | Nicholls, Archibald |
| 8 | Davis, Leonard | 46 | Fisher, Martin | 85 | Nicholls, Ninian |
| 9 | Wilson, Jonathan, Feb. 7th | 47 | Pritchett, William | 86 | Barber, Samuel* |
| 10 | Magruder, Zaak | 48 | Williams, William, Jr. | 87 | Williams, William, Sr. |
| 11 | Brooke, Richard | 49 | Beans, Christopher | 88 | Beckwith, John |
| 12 | Crampkin, Thos. Jr. | 50 | Beall, Clement | 89 | Harbin, Joshua |
| 13 | Magruder, John B., 1778, | 51 | Orme, James | 90 | Magruder, Nathan |
| | Feb. 7th. | 52 | Allison, Thomas | 91 | Williams, Amos |
| 14 | Crabb, Richard | 53 | Allison, Jonathan* | 92 | Williams, Charles |
| 15 | Woolton, Richard | 54 | Dod, James | 93 | Beckwith, William, Feb. |
| 16 | Whitaker, Alexa. | 55 | Benjamin, Abram* Feb. | | 28, 1778. |
| 17 | Williams, Elisha Owen | | 24, 1778. | 94 | Prather, Aaron |
| 18 | Griffith, Chas. Gray | 56 | Bayne, Balter | 95 | Magruder, Isaac |
| 19 | Howe, Paul | 57 | Butt, Rignuld* | 96 | Watson, Henry |
| 20 | Casey, Philip | 58 | Ricketts, Benjamin, Jr. | 97 | Prather, Azariah |
| 21 | Onaill, William | 59 | Brome, John | 98 | Randell, John |
| 22 | Nichols, Benjamin, 10th | 60 | Sansbury, Thomas* | 99 | Allison, John* |
| | Feb. (of Wm.) | 61 | Dyar, Thomas | 100 | Coyl, Samuel |
| 23 | Sisilend, William | 62 | Allison, Benjamin* | 101 | Colgan, Michael |
| 24 | Elock, Robt. | 63 | Brome, Peter* | 102 | Nicholls, Samuel |
| 25 | West, William (of John) | 64 | Nicholls, Edward | 103 | Dowe, Robt. |
| 26 | West, Basil | 65 | Burton, Joseph | 104 | Coyl, Charles* |
| 27 | West, Osborn | 66 | Griffith, Hezh. | 105 | Perry, James |
| 28 | Casey, Leven | 67 | Watts, John | 106 | Reintzel, Andrew |
| 29 | Peack, Lewis | 68 | Kirk, Thomas | 107 | Beckwith, Basil |
| 30 | Offutt, Nathl. (of Sam.) | 69 | Busey, Edward | 108 | Ricketts, Jacob* |
| 31 | West, Benjamin | 70 | Busey, Paul* | 109 | Tole, Stephen* |
| 32 | West, Joseph, Jr. | 71 | Chapman, William | 110 | Swerarringer, Thomas |
| 33 | Offutt, Saml. Owen | 72 | Rhoades, Jacob | 111 | Hadley, James |
| 34 | Beall, James (of Ninn.) | 73 | Chew, Joseph | 112 | Crofford, Nathaniel, Feb. |
| | Feb. 21st, 1778. | 74 | Hinton, John* Feb. 26, | | 28, 1778. |
| 35 | Clarke, William | | 1778. | 113 | Low, Patrick |
| 36 | Offutt, William Mackle | 75 | West, Joseph* | 114 | Crofford, Robert Beall |
| 37 | Peack, Benj. | 76 | Rhoades, John* | 115 | Willett, Benjamin |
| 38 | Baily, Nicholas | 77 | Busey, Charles* | 116 | Allison, Richard |
| 39 | Hurdle, Lawrence | 78 | Lozenby, John | 117 | Hawker, Amberos* |

| | | |
|---|---|---|
| 118 Tomson, Zackh.* | 134 Reintzel, Jacob | 150 Callihan, Richard* |
| 119 Dunn, Thomas* | 135 Lowery, William | 151 Crofford, John Sutton |
| 120 Onaill, John* | 136 Boyd, William | 152 Warger, Richd.* |
| 121 Butt, Richard* | 137 Stoner, Jacob | 153 Hews, Nathl.* |
| 122 Lannom, Ralph* | 138 Boyd, John | 154 Lucker, Stephen* |
| 123 Stewart, Mordecai | 139 Prather, Walter | 155 Shaw, John* |
| 124 Dyer, Samuel | 140 Prater, Zaccai | 156 Adams, Alexd. |
| 125 Sweny, Owen* | 141 Holland, Thomas* | 157 Allison, Richd.* |
| 126 Williams, John* | 142 Jones, John* | 158 Peach, James* |
| 127 Pritchett, Charles* | 143 Lowmen, Thomas* | 159 Duckett, Isaac* |
| 128 Allison, Charles* | 144 Gatton, William | 160 Willson, Alexa. |
| 129 Smith, Nicholas,* Feb. 28, | 145 Anderson, John | 161 Perry, Chas. |
| 1778. | 146 Boyd, Abraham | 162 Ricketts, Thomas |
| 130 Harriss, Nathan | 147 Gatton, Richd. | 163 Carnole, Samuel |
| 131 Suter, James | 148 Gatton, Zackariah | 164 Green, William* |
| 132 Bailey, John, Jr | 149 Griffith, George, Feb. 28th, | 165 Robertson, Wm. |
| 133 Maquess, John | 1778. | |

In submission to the General Assembly of Maryland Relative to an Act passed at a late Session in regard to Taking the Oath of Affirmation of Fidelity and Support to this State; I do Certify that all these afsd Subscribers have voluntarily made their Personel Appearance before me one of the Majestrates of Montgomery County and have taken and repeated the afsd Prefixed Oath as afsd and Subscribed their names and marks thereto agreeable to directions of said act. Given under my hand this 2nd day of March A. D. 1778.

JOSEPH WILSON.

1   *The Worshipful William Deakins', Jr., Returns.*

| | | |
|---|---|---|
| 2 Beall, Zepheniah | 33 Reynolds, William | 65 Tucker, John (son of |
| 3 Beall, Nin | 34 Tucker, John | Edwd.) |
| 4 Darby, Asa | 35 Buckland, John | 66 Dowden, Zepheniah |
| 5 Read, John | 36 Martin, Samuel | 67 Winson, Isaac |
| 6 Dougherty, John | 37 Gazaway, Charles | 68 Tracy, Charles |
| 7 Greenwell, Bennett | 38 Smith, Samuel | 69 Broadack, Joseph |
| 8 Chilton, Sturman | 39 Kirby, Enock | 70 Cook, Richard |
| 9 Ray, Benjamin | 40 Allphin, Edward | 71 Pancoast, Oden |
| 10 Offutt, Samuel | 41 Watkins, John, Jr. | 72 Countz, Henry |
| 11 Gilksy, Samuel | 42 Blackmore, William | 73 Roberts, Richard |
| 12 Dove, Benjamin | 43 Mills, Jessee | 74 Denniss, William |
| 13 Clagett, Alexander | 44 Nicholls, Thomas | 75 McDaniel, Elisha |
| 14 Noe, Peter | 45 Dowden, Thomas, Jr. | 76 Elliott, Mark |
| 15 Beall, Thomas (of George) | 46 Nicholls, Thomas, Jr. | 77 Walter, Clement |
| 16 Beall, Alexander | 47 Holmes, John | 78 Fife, Abijah |
| 17 Tracy, Alexander | 48 Dowden, Zachariah | 79 Broadhead, Thomas |
| 18 Barnes, John | 49 Clark, Richard | 80 Doron, John |
| 19 Beall, Leven | 50 Clark, Clement | 81 Tucker, Jonathan |
| 20 Mockebee, John | 51 Clark, Edward | 82 Brown, William |
| 21 Clagett, John, Jr. | 52 Smith, Peter | 83 Pelly, James |
| 22 Ward, Benjamin (of | 53 Waters, James | 84 Moore, James |
| Joseph) | 54 Thompson, John | 85 Adair, William |
| 23 Wowden, Michael | 55 Campbell, John | 86 Drake, Robert |
| 24 Butler, Tobias | 56 Evans, William | 87 Chambers, James |
| 25 Sherbutt, Thomas | 57 Chambers, Henry | 88 Arnold, Josephas |
| 26 Dyson, Maddox | 58 Jones, Thomas | 89 Allison, James |
| 27 McDade, Daniel | 59 Therlkeld, Joseph | 90 Dowing, Francis |
| 28 Barnes, Joseph | 60 Fields, John | 91 Freeman, Richard |
| 29 Bragg, William | 61 Murphy, Darby | 92 Harper, Francis |
| 30 Brown, William | 62 Chambers, William | 93 Harper, Francis, Jr. |
| 31 Orme, Archd. | 63 McKintosh, Alexander | 94 Clifford, Hugh |
| 32 Stephens, Michael | 64 Thompson, William | |

STATE OF MARYLAND, MONTGOMERY COUNTY, March 3d, 1778.

I do hereby Certify that the aforegoing List is a just and true Copy of the Book kept by me for the purpose of Administering the Oath of Fidelity and Support to this State, and that the persons therein mentioned have taken repeated and Subscribed the said Oath.

WILL DEAKINS, JNR.

## 1  *The Worshipfull Joseph Offutt's Returns.*

2   Magruder, Joseph
3   Offutt, Mordecia
4   Jones, Charles
5   Murphy, John
6   Murphy, Charles
7   Maguire, Andrew
8   Tannihill, Ninian
9   Offutt, William
10  Offutt, Zadox
11  Grant, William
12  Dent, John
13  Offutt, William, Jr.
14  Beall Robert (son of N.)
15  Murphey, William
16  Evans, Joseph
17  Offutt, Nathaniel, Jr.
18  Bealle, Thomas
19  Beall, Bazil

20  Offutt, Thomas
21  English, King
22  Offutt, Rezin
23  Offutt, James, Feb. 6, 1778.
24  Fleming, John
25  Offutt, William the 3rd
26  Shields, Thomas
27  Offutt, Thomas, Sr.
28  Childs, Henry
29  Hitch John
30  Hamilton, David
31  Clagett, Samuel, Feb. 13, 1778.
32  Jarboe, Stephen
33  Fleming, James
34  Tucker, Jacob
35  Offutt, George H.
36  Offutt, Hezekiah

37  Brown, John
38  Hedly, Jacob
39  Remington, John
40  Hopkins, Richard
41  Harp, William
42  Culph, George
43  Scott, Thomas
44  Fleming, John, Jr.
45  Speak, Richard
46  Duley, John
47  Speak, Ignatius
48  Sutherland, Alexander
49  Wilson, John
50  Haislip, James
51  Edmonston, Maccuben
52  Viley, George
53  Eads, Edward
54  Bogler, John

MONTGOMERY COUNTY, March 2d, 1778.

True Copy from the original before me.

JOSEPH OFFUTT.

## 1  *The Worshipfull Charles Jones' Returns, Jan. 10, 1778.*

2   Lyon, David
3   Thomas, Robert
4   Belt, Joseph Sprigg
5   Jones, Henry
6   Gettings, Thomas
7   Tracy, Philip
8   Williams, Daniel
9   Barrett, John
10  Street, John
11  Housley, Robert
12  Gettings, Benjn.
13  Barrett Ninian
14  Willmutt, Thomas
15  Forwhoaler, Frans.
16  Barnes, Josiah
17  Whelan, Nicholas
18  Nicholson, Richard
19  Harwood, Samuel
20  Beall, Thadous
21  Gettings, Basil
22  Barrett, Benj.
23  Whitehead, Timothy
24  Read, George
25  Jones, Charles
26  McDaniel, John
27  Harrison, James
28  Marshall, James
29  Greaves, Thos.
30  Johns, Thos.
31  Beall, Samuel, Jr.
32  Beall, Joseph Belt
33  Bagly, William
34  Stewart, Brain

35  Orme, Moses
36  Orme, Phillip
37  Reynolds, Chas.
38  Maccubbin, Thos.
39  Carroll, Daniel, Jr.
40  Wilcoxon, Lewis
41  Nevett, James
42  Nicholls, Thos.
43  Jadson, John
44  Higgins, James
45  Orme, Ellry
46  Prather, Baruch
47  Whelan, Mathew
48  Loadon, Nichols
49  Connoly, Thos.
50  Connoly, John
51  Connoly, Michael
52  Carroll, Rev. J.
53  Trout, Edmund
54  Keiser, John
55  Keiser, Christn.
56  Keiser, Michal
57  Mardon, John
58  Beall, Robt.
59  Harris, Aaron
60  Boardon, John
61  Harris Zadock
62  Trundel, John
63  Harris, Zadock
64  Beall, Richard
65  Cookontofft, Michael
66  Cookontofft, Stofol

67  Bowie, Allen
68  Silver, Nathanell
69  Beall, Thos.
70  Bloyss, David
71  Busey, Joshua
72  Goodrick, Benjamin
73  Busey, John
74  Busey, Samuel
75  Graves, Peter
76  Slicer, James
77  Topping, James
78  Lanham, Aaron
79  Pritchott, Elias
80  Mockeby, Zacha
81  Woods, William
82  Beezley, Mosses
83  Smith, David
84  Jones, Henry
85  Mochbe, Zepha
86  Speaks, Hezekiah
87  Chappell, Thomas
88  Roberson, Nathan
89  Whelan, Mathew
90  Jennings, John
91  Glays, William
92  Maccubbin, Zackh.
93  Shoomaker, Joshua
94  Evans, Zachariah
95  Trundel, Josiah
96  Whelan, Michal
97  Buckley, John
98  Farrall, John

A true Copy.
CHARLES JONES.

## 1 *The Worshipfull Samuel W. Magruder's Returns.*

| | | |
|---|---|---|
| 2 Magruder, Levin | 47 Moor, Elisha* | 93 Bentin, William |
| 3 Talbott, William | 48 Lewis, Thomas | 94 Wallace, James, Jr. |
| 4 Flint, Thomas | 49 Sparrow, Benj.* | 95 Wallace, Nathl. |
| 5 Beiraft, Peter | 50 Ball, John | 96 Young, Peter* |
| 6 Woodward, Benedict | 51 Abington, John | 97 Clagett, John |
| 7 Dorsey, Greenburry | 52 Tracy, Wm. | 98 Steall, William* |
| 8 Riley, Ninian | 53 Ball, James | 99 Edmonston, Thos. |
| 9 Magruder, Nathl. (ofNinian) | 54 Ball, John Sr. | 100 Mackebee, James |
| 10 Johnson, John | 55 Baker, John* | 101 Wallace, William |
| 11 Johnson, John | 56 Collyar, William | 102 Awbery, William |
| 12 Magruder, Elias | 57 Magruder, Ninian | 103 Harris, Bartin B. |
| 13 Magruder, Zachariah | 58 Harris, Nathn. | 104 Duley, Thomas* |
| 14 Beall, George ye 3rd | 59 Maholl, Stephen* | 105 Clements, William |
| 15 Olel, Barruch | 60 Duley, James* | 106 Ward, John |
| 16 Sparrow, Thomas | 61 Jones, William | 107 Smith, James* |
| 17 Sparrow, William* | 62 Foulton, Robt.* | 108 Higdon, Thomas, Jr. |
| 18 Greenfield Walter S. | 63 Barber, John | 109 Magruder, Ninian Beall |
| 19 Brook, Isaac | 64 Sparrow, Jonahan* | 110 Beall, Zachariah |
| 20 Clagett, Nathan | 65 Allison, Hezekiah | 111 Young, Abraham |
| 21 White, Joseph | 66 Stevens, John | 112 Clagett, Joseph |
| 22 Magruder, Wm. Beall | 67 Glase, Joseph | 113 Willitt, William |
| 23 Magruder, Josiah | 68 Jones, Evan | 114 Willitt, Ninian |
| 24 Herring, John | 69 Maddox, Thomas | 115 Wallace, William |
| 25 Magruder, Wm. Offutt | 70 Preast, Henry* | 116 Ridgway, Isaac* |
| 26 Moore, James | 71 Magruder, Samuel B. | 117 Loodge, William |
| 27 Riley, Hugh | 72 Taylar, Walter* | 118 Jones, Evan, Jr.* |
| 28 Benton, Joseph* | 73 Ray, James* | 119 Magruder, Archabald |
| 29 Blocklock, Richd. | 74 Adams, Alexa. | 120 Price, Richd. |
| 30 Adams, Edward | 75 Harris, Benjamin | 121 Magruder, John |
| 31 Auston, John | 76 Moor, Barton | 122 Gettings, Benjamin |
| 32 Wallace, Zephaniah | 77 Duckett, Samuel | 123 Sharlock, James |
| 33 Magruder, Normond Bruce | 78 Duley, James* | 124 Chamber, Wm. T. |
| 34 Woodard, John* | 79 Stiles, William* | 125 Auston, Alex.* |
| 35 Magruder, Saml. Brewer | 80 Maholl, Samuel* | 126 Magruder, Walter |
| 36 Mufphel, Barney' | 81 Magruder, Edward | 127 Wiliams, Elisha* |
| 37 Mag,uder, Enoch | 82 Collyar, William, Jr. | 128 Harris, George |
| 38 Watson, John | 83 Benton, Benjamin S. | 129 Miles, Thomas |
| 39 Early, Benjamin | 84 Sedwick, John | 130 Tucker, William* |
| 40 Locker, John* | 85 Dezelm, Moses* | 131 Shehorn, James* |
| 41 Wilcoxson, Jesse | 86 Coventry, Chas. | 132 Wallace, Harburt |
| 42 Cheshire, Burch | 87 Fardo, John Lewis | 133 Lemonar, John |
| 43 Litton, Michael | 88 Magruder, Richd. | 134 Heughs, Edward |
| 44 Jones, Chars. (son of Joh.) | 89 Sedwick, William* | 135 Magruder, Nathaniel (of Arch) |
| 45 Cheshese, John | 90 Elder, Hugh | |
| 46 Wilson, Zedekiah* | 91 King, Samuel* | |
| | 92 Jones, Nathn.* | |

A true Copy.

## SAMUEL W. MAGRUDER.

## 1 *The Worshipfull Richard Thompson's Returns.*

| | | |
|---|---|---|
| 2 Turner, Samuel | 19 Beall, George, Jr. | 36 Bignell, Robert |
| 3 McFadon, Alexander | 20 Wise, John | 37 Keyser, Frederick |
| 4 Belt, Joseph | 21 Evans, Samuel | 38 Nicholls, James |
| 5 Duvall, Mareen | 22 Doull, James | 39 Threlkeld, Henry |
| 6 Jones, William | 23 Swarigen, Van | 40 Williamson, Alexander |
| 7 Rigden, Thomas | 24 Barrett, Thomas | 41 Magruder, Samuel ye 3rd |
| 8 Clagett, John, Sr. | 25 Cecil, Samuel | 42 Cecil, John |
| 9 Chappell, John | 26 Gassler, Anthony | 43 Moone, William |
| 10 Threlkeld, John | 27 Holmead, Anthony | 44 Heugh, Andrew |
| 11 Moss, Francis | 28 Clark, Henry | 45 Clevely, Henry |
| 12 Beall, George | 29 Cecil, Sabrat | 46 Garlick, Joseph |
| 13 Magruder, Hezekiah | 30 Wetzel, Frederick | 47 Parker, William |
| 14 Nicholls, William | 31 Hess, Jacob | 48 Peter, Robert, Jr. |
| 15 Daly, John | 32 Kraus, Theodorus | 49 Hell, John |
| 16 Gibhart, John | 33 Boerhaane, Valentine | 50 Hoffman, Martin |
| 17 Reitzel, Valentine | 34 Reintzel, Daniel | 51 Ray, Thomas |
| 18 Murdock, John | 35 Becraft, Benjamin, Jr. | 52 Day, Leonard |

| 53 | Thompson, William |
| 54 | Stewart, Wm. Veale |
| 55 | Kersner, Michael |
| 56 | Langton, James |
| 57 | Gillham, Thomas |
| 58 | Crown, Lancelot |
| 59 | Crawford, Thomas |
| 60 | Purdey, Charles |
| 61 | Carter, William |
| 62 | Slack, John |
| 63 | Carman, Thomas |
| 64 | Peter, Robert |
| 65 | Wallace, James |
| 66 | Hopkins, John, Jr. |
| 67 | Moss, Robert |
| 68 | Clagett, Richard Keene |
| 69 | Smith, Walter |
| 70 | Leyle, John |
| 71 | Huth, Samuel |
| 72 | Clark, Herman |
| 73 | Kurtz, Nicholas |
| 74 | Magrath, William |
| 75 | Doyl, Richard |
| 76 | Roughside, William |
| 77 | Grabber, Philip |
| 78 | Murphy, William |
| 79 | Brandish, Thomas |
| 80 | Talburtt, John |
| 81 | Fowler, Elisha |
| 82 | Beall, John |
| 83 | Pearce, Benjamin Notley |
| 84 | McCabe, Henry, Jr. |
| 85 | Baker, William |
| 86 | White, Alexander |
| 87 | Long, James |
| 88 | Garner, Paul |
| 89 | Dombach, Frederick |
| 90 | Bisbin, James |
| 91 | Manning, James |
| 92 | Yates, Josiah |
| 93 | O'Brien, Philip |
| 94 | Kogenderfer, Frederick |
| 95 | Kogenderfer, Leonard |
| 96 | Trissler, Jacob |
| 97 | Middogh, John |
| 98 | Mounts, John |
| 99 | Paull, Nicholas |
| 100 | Weynberger, George |
| 101 | Yost, John |
| 102 | Howes, John |
| 103 | Beall, Josiah |
| 104 | Fetherkeyl, George Michael |
| 105 | Eppracht, Jacob |
| 106 | Legenberger, Nicholas |
| 107 | Boerhaave, Simon |
| 108 | McFardon, Samuel |
| 109 | Ingram, Thomas |
| 110 | Reisner, Jacob |
| 111 | McFardon, Joseph |

A List of the names of Sundry Persons Inhabitants of Montgomery County, who have taken the Oath of Fidelity and Support of the State of Maryland before

RICHARD THOMPSON.

For the Governor and Council of Maryland.

1  *The Worshipfull Oneas Campbell's Returns.*

| 2 | Luckett, William |
| 3 | Jacobs, Jeremiah |
| 4 | Scott, Charles* |
| 5 | McCleary, John |
| 6 | McDeakens, Leonard |
| 7 | Fenemore, William |
| 8 | Warmer, Samuel, Sr. |
| 9 | Catol, William |
| 10 | Wellett, Griffith |
| 11 | Dode, Daniel* |
| 12 | Shearbutt, Samuel* |
| 13 | Warner, Thomas |
| 14 | Askey, Zachariah |
| 15 | Ellis, Zachariah |
| 16 | Green, Bendick |
| 17 | Donaldson, Alexander |
| 18 | Myre, Conrad* |
| 19 | McTel, Samuel |
| 20 | Jones, Philip |
| 21 | Johnson, Barholomew |
| 22 | Hickman, Arthur |
| 23 | Heagerty, James |
| 24 | McGinnis, Neale* |
| 25 | Beachmore, Samuel |
| 26 | Lewis, John |
| 27 | Griffith, Charles (of Harry) |
| 28 | Green, Philip |
| 29 | Furguson, Joseph |
| 30 | Walter, George |
| 31 | Walters, Levy |
| 32 | Watkins Leonard |
| 33 | Nobb, John* |
| 34 | Sears, William |
| 35 | Veatch, Richd. |
| 36 | Sears, James* |
| 37 | Biggs, Samuel |
| 38 | Sibley, James |
| 39 | Shutleworth, Philip |
| 40 | Pe Deeomtz (Pe De Comtz?), Nicholas |
| 41 | Barkley, Charles |
| 42 | Jamline, Grove* |
| 43 | Ellis, Shederick |
| 44 | Wynn, Robert |
| 45 | Harwood, John |
| 46 | Jones, Edward |
| 47 | Belt, Carlton |
| 48 | Williams, John |
| 49 | Gatton, James |
| 50 | Burn, Mathais |
| 51 | Hoskinson, George |
| 52 | Allison, Hendrey |
| 53 | Newman Benjamin* |
| 54 | Bowen, John* |
| 55 | Kiser, Martin |
| 56 | Lazenby, Robert |
| 57 | Smith, Stephen |
| 58 | Lazenby, Thomas |
| 59 | Cartwright, Thomas |
| 60 | Taylor, John |
| 61 | Campbell, John, Jr. |
| 62 | Hickman, Elitrue |
| 63 | Sanders, Charles |
| 64 | Lucas, William* |
| 65 | Oliver, William* |
| 66 | Stephens, Lewis |
| 67 | Chilton, James |
| 68 | Cartwright, Samuel |
| 69 | Wheeler, John Hanson |
| 70 | Davis, Baxley |
| 71 | Green, John* |
| 72 | Naylor, Joshua |
| 73 | Hagan, Micheal* |
| 74 | Green, Isaac |
| 75 | Newman, Jacob* |
| 76 | Campbell, James |
| 77 | Hunter, Joshua* |
| 78 | Steep, Arthur* |
| 79 | Thomas, Martin* |
| 80 | Riggs, Thomas Wheelen |
| 81 | Riggs, Azeriah* |
| 82 | Riggs, Benjamin* |
| 83 | Rayon, John |
| 84 | Miles, John |
| 85 | Lucas, Charles |
| 86 | Moxley, Daniel |
| 87 | Adams, Jasse |
| 88 | Moxley, John |
| 89 | Gatton, Benjamin |
| 90 | Woodard, William* |
| 91 | Wilkinson, William* |
| 92 | Yates, Ignatus |
| 93 | Chilton, Thomas |
| 94 | Chilton, Marke* |
| 95 | Jones, Daniel |
| 96 | Colier, William |
| 97 | Hutts, Andrew* |
| 98 | Geats, James |
| 99 | Davis, Isaiah* |
| 100 | Davis, Ephraim* |
| 101 | Robie, John Tayler* |
| 102 | Sears, James* |
| 103 | McGlocklon, Henry* |
| 104 | Fletcher, Thomas |
| 105 | Hickman, William, Jr. |
| 106 | Hickman, William |
| 107 | Henley, James |
| 108 | Burn, Adam |

109  *The Worshipfull James Hutts—No Returns.*

The above Persons were Sworn before me at Sundry times, Returns the 31st Jan. and the 2nd March, 1778. Given under my hand and Seal this 3rd March, 1778.

ONS. CAMPBELL  [SEAL]

1 *The Worshipfull Thomas Sprigg Wooton's Returns.*

2 Offutt, Alexander      4 Offutt, Zehaniah      5 Crabb, John
3 White, John

MONTG. COUNTY, March 3rd, 1778.

True Copy from the Original Book.

THOS. SPRIGG WOOTON.

To his Excellency Thomas Johnson, Esq., Governor of Maryland.

1 *The Worshipfull Elisha William's Returns.*

| | | |
|---|---|---|
| 2 Patrick, William | 56 Sprigg, Thomas | 110 Viers, Elijah |
| 3 Wood, Stephen | 57 Hays, William | 111 Allnutt, Lawrence |
| 4 Dyson, Barton | 58 Hays, George | 112 Allnutt, Jesse |
| 5 Chiswell, Stephen N. | 59 Williamson, William | 113 Allnutt, James, Jr. |
| 6 Clagett, Ninian | 60 Clagett, Henry | 114 Allnutt, William |
| 7 Dowden, Thomas | 61 Riggs, John | 115 Allnutt, John |
| 8 Godman, Humphry | 62 White, Samuel | 116 Darnal, John |
| 9 Dowden, John | 63 Harris, Norris | 117 O'Neal, Laurence |
| 10 Jacob, Joseph | 64 Talbott, Thomas | 118 Neal, Charles |
| 11 Hardy, John | 65 Wayman, Thomas | 119 Hungerford, Charles |
| 12 Poole, Joseph | 66 Harris, Nathan | 120 Henry, Daniel |
| 13 Hemsear, Mathias | 67 Maddin, Jonathan, Jr. | 121 Sinclair, Duncan |
| 14 Ray, William | 68 Maddin, Jonathan, Sr. | 122 Robertson, John |
| 15 Nabours, Nahan | 69 Stephens, Edward | 123 Harding, Walter |
| 16 Plummer, Jeremiah | 70 Maddin, Richard | 124 Dyson, Zephaniah |
| 17 Reed, Jonathan | 71 Maddin, John | 125 Smith, Charles |
| 18 Reed, Mathew | 72 Norris, William | 126 Tomlinson, William |
| 19 McDeed, Patrick | 73 Harris, John | 127 Smith, Nathan |
| 20 Walker, William | 74 Patrick, John | 128 Fyffe, Joseph |
| 21 Hunter, Henry | 75 Warren, George | 129 Cawood, Stephen |
| 22 McDavit, James | 76 Thomson, John Baptist | 130 Warren, Thomas, Sr. |
| 23 Hemsear, Christian | 77 Coats, Charles | 131 Warren, George |
| 24 Smith, Richard | 78 Owen, John | 132 Allnutt, James, Sr. |
| 25 Norris, George | 79 Clagett, Charles | 133 Warren, John |
| 26 White, Walter | 80 Magruder, James | 134 Belt, Higginson |
| 27 Hays, Charles | 81 Clagett, John | 135 Street, Francis |
| 28 Chiswell, Joseph N. | 82 Wheelan, Daniel | 136 Michill, Benjamin |
| 29 Reader, Simon | 83 Warmans, Stephen | 137 Dawson, Thomas |
| 30 Wood, Aristarchus | 84 Jerre, Alexander | 138 Wilson, Mathew |
| 31 Floskinson, Hugh | 85 Howard, Thomas | 139 Veaes, Daniel |
| 32 Custer, Christian | 86 Miller, Thomas | 140 Dawson, Nicholas |
| 33 Murphey, Frances | 87 Burdit, Nathan | 141 Darby, Benjamin |
| 34 Jones, John the 3rd | 88 Green, Raphel | 142 Hoker, Samuel |
| 35 Seaborn, John | 89 Hays, Thomas | 143 Dawson, Benoni |
| 36 Coats, Notly | 90 Simpson, James | 144 Taul, Arthur Thomas |
| 37 Norris, Benjamin | 91 Green, Samuel | 145 Roberts, Zephaniah |
| 38 Sprigg, James | 92 Mitchaell, Robert | 146 McDaniel, William, Sr. |
| 39 Javett, William | 93 Hall, Alexander | 147 McDaniel, William, Jr. |
| 40 Sprigg, Frederick | 94 Hays, Leaven | 148 Wilcockson, Henry |
| 41 Ennis, John | 95 Hays, Jeremiah, Jr. | 149 Wilson, John |
| 42 Tomlinson, Humphry B. | 96 Hays, Jeremiah, Sr. | 150 Dawson, Robert Doyne |
| 43 Wyvill, Edward Hale | 97 Love, Thomas | 151 Veatch, Thomas |
| 44 McDeed, Robt. | 98 Warman, Stephen, Jr. | 152 Wallace, William |
| 45 Crager, Laurence | 99 Nott, Zachariah | 153 Love, Leonard |
| 46 McKay, William | 100 Hagan, Leonard | 154 Roberts, James |
| 47 Young, John | 101 Howard, William | 155 Power, Nicholas |
| 48 Walker, Robert | 102 Summers, John | 156 Love, Samuel |
| 49 Veatch, Nathan | 103 Summers, William, Sr. | 157 Wayman, Leonard |
| 50 Wilson, Wadsworth | 104 Summers, Thomas | 158 Purdy, Richard |
| 51 Harris, Joseph | 105 Summers, William, Jr. | 159 Fyffe, James, Sr. |
| 52 Hays, Charles, Sr. | 106 Nezbit, Charles | 160 Ellis, Samuel |
| 53 Hays, Basil | 107 Nezbit, Bernard | 161 Dowel, Peter |
| 54 Harris, Jesse | 108 Wilson, Robert | 162 Lanham, John |
| 55 Veatch, Hezekiah | 109 Viers, William | 163 Loveless, Benjamin |

| | | | | | | | |
|---|---|---|---|---|---|---|---|
| 164 | Stimpson, Solloman | 180 | Higdon, Joseph | 196 | Soper, James |
| 165 | Watson, Samuel | 181 | Higdon, John | 197 | Veatch, Ninian |
| 166 | Tomblinson, Hugh | 182 | Dowel, Richard | 198 | Speight, Robert |
| 167 | Loveless, Elkanah | 183 | Wood, Zephaniah | 199 | Thomas, William |
| 168 | Ellis, Zephiniah | 184 | Locker, Shadrick | 200 | Ellis, Solomon |
| 169 | Watson, Elkanah | 185 | Fyffe, James | 201 | Jones, Joseph |
| 170 | Hardy, Zadock | 186 | Talbot, Notly | 202 | Wood, John |
| 171 | Johnson, Isaac | 187 | Harbin, Joshua | 203 | McDaniel, Henry |
| 172 | Meeks, George | 188 | O'Neal, Peter | 204 | Hoskinson, Charles |
| 173 | Willson, Thomas | 189 | Fyffe, Jonathan | 205 | Ros, John |
| 174 | Loveless, Barton | 190 | Gibson, John | 206 | Dowel, Philip |
| 175 | Speake, Charles | 191 | Veatch, John | 207 | Dowel, John |
| 176 | Veatch, Ninean | 192 | Lirnold, William | 208 | Swann, Zephoneah |
| 177 | Speak, Nathan | 193 | Douglass, Samuel | 209 | Oliver, Laurence |
| 178 | Draper, John | 194 | Walter, David | 210 | Robertson, James |
| 179 | Talbot, Basil | 195 | Ellis, Joshua | | |

For His Excellency the Governor and Council.

March 2d, 1778.

ELISHA WILLIAMS.

---

## OATH OF FIDELITY AND SUPPORT
## REQUIRED FROM CIVIL OFFICERS, MONTGOMERY COUNTY, MD.,
### 1780-1782.

Contributed by C. C. Magruder, Jr., Esq., Upper Marlboro, Prince George's County, Md.*

I, A. B., do swear I do not hold myself bound to yield any Allegiance or obedience to the King of Great Britain his heirs or Successors and that I will be true and faithful to the State of Maryland and will to the utmost of my power, Support maintain and defend the Freedom and Independence thereof and the Government as Now Established against all open enemies and secret and Traiterous Conspiracies and will use my utmost endeavours to disclose and make Known to the Government or some one of The judges or Justices Thereof all treasons or Traiterous Conspiracies attempts of Combinations against This State or the government Thereof which may come to my knowledge so help me God.

| | | | | | |
|---|---|---|---|---|---|
| | *February 9th, 1780.* | 15 | Ross, David, Atty. | 31 | Brookes, Walton |
| 1 | Jones, Charles | 16 | Cryer, Thomas Nicholls* | 32 | Dorsey, Walter |
| 2 | Burgess, Edward | 17 | Dorsey, W. H. | 33 | Hunt, William P. |
| 3 | Wilson, Joseph | 18 | Nicholls, Edward | 34 | Wallace, William |
| | *March 13th, 1780.* | 19 | Gantt, Jno. M. | 35 | Gaither, Elijah |
| 4 | Offutt, Jas. | 20 | Gantt, Erasmus | 36 | Owing, William |
| 5 | Thompson, Richard | 21 | Perry, James, Coroner | 37 | Beall, Brooke |
| 6 | Campbell, Ans | 22 | Lowndes, Richd. F. | 38 | Neill, Bernard O. |
| 7 | Wootton, T. Sprigg | 23 | Jones, Benja. W. | 39 | Threlkile, John |
| 8 | Martin, Luther | 24 | Holmes, Josiah | 40 | Samto, Thomas |
| 9 | Holmes, John | 25 | Wayman, John Junior | 41 | Rientzel, Valentine |
| 10 | Caton, Charles | 26 | Nelson, R. | 42 | Gardiner, James |
| 11 | Wilson, Thomas O. | 27 | Martin, Lenox | 43 | Selby, Sam 3rd |
| 12 | Ridgely, H., Jr., Atty. | 28 | Hall, Richard | 44 | Williams, Robert |
| | *March 13th, 1782.* | 29 | Magruder, Patrick | 45 | Linsted, Tho. |
| 13 | Wootton, Richd. | | *22 July* | | |
| 14 | Smith, Rob, Atty. | 30 | Magruder, George | | |

### THE FOLLOWING QUALIFIED FOR JUSTICES OF THE PEACE IN MONTGOMERY COUNTY, MARYLAND:

| | | | | | |
|---|---|---|---|---|---|
| | *February 9, 1780* | | *March 13, 1780* | | |
| 46 | Jones, Charles | 49 | Offutt, Js. | 52 | Holmes, John |
| 47 | Burgess, Edward | 50 | Thompson, Richard | 53 | Wootton, Richard |
| 48 | Wilson, Joseph | 51 | Campbell, Ens. | | |

( Montgomery County Test Book, 1780.)

---

* "It is patent from the records that the persons named in this list subscribed to the Oath as a condition precedent to their assumption of some Civil Office, but what office is not clear except as therein indicated. * * * Certainly no question of duress or mental reservation can arise * * * for the loyalty of such subscribers must have been well known, otherwise they would not have been considered eligible for Civil Offices"—Feb. 13, 1917.                                                    C. C. M., JR.

## WASHINGTON COUNTY, MARYLAND

### PATRIOT'S OATH, MARCH COURT, 1778.

"A List of Persons in Washington County Who Have Taken the Following Oath Before the Different Magistrates Mentioned Below; and Returned by Them to Washington County Court."

I hereby Certify that the following persons have taken the Oath of Fidelity and Support to the State of Maryland agreeable to the Act Entitled An Act for the better Security to the Government. Given under my hand this 1st Mch., 1778.

SAM HUGHES.

Washington County was established in 1776 from Frederick County.

The "Oath of Fidelity and Support" is reproduced upon page 1 of this number.

Thirteen Returns, 1485 men. Recorded Maryland Historical Society—copy from copy of original. Published through the courtesy and cooperation of those mentioned upon page 1.

*The Worshipfull Sam Hughes' Returns.*

| | | |
|---|---|---|
| 1 Walling, James, Sr. | 16 Hicson, Joseph | 30 Fleck, John |
| 2 Gaither, Henry | 17 Warkin, Peter | 31 Reiley, John |
| 3 Macnabb, John | 18 Perry, Daniel | 32 Gaither, Richard |
| 4 Fallnos, William | 19 Carpenter, John | 33 McClellan, Robert |
| 5 Duggan, Thomas | 20 Allender, Richard | 34 Ekell, Christian |
| 6 Brown, Simon | 21 Charlton, Thomas | 35 Lee, William |
| 7 Williams, James | 22 Beggs, Andrew | 36 McClosker, Stephen |
| 8 Dunn, Thomas | 23 Hoffman, George | 37 Funk, Jacob |
| 9 Coliflower, George, Jr. | 24 Harr, Adam | 38 Funk, John |
| 10 Coliflower, Nichael | 25 Clark, James | 39 Sprigg, Osborn |
| 11 Monroe, Barney | 26 Adair, John | 40 Brandenburgh, Christopher |
| 12 Simkins, William | 27 Gillepie, James | 41 Thompson, John |
| 13 Huet, Nicholas | 28 Con, John | 42 Adair, James |
| 14 Mony, Adam, Jr. | 29 Norwood, Belt | 43 Campbell, Benjamin |
| 15 McAdele, Patrick | | |

*The Worshipfull Chrs. Cruso's Returns.*

A True Copy of the Free Male Taxibils of Sharpsburgh and Lower Antietam Hundred. I do hereby Certify that the hereafter foloing hath Voluntarily taken and Subscribed to Oath of Allegience and Fidelity as Directed by an Act of the General Assembly of the State of Maryland Passed the 5th day of Feb. 1777.

Witness my hand and Seal the 2d Day of March, 1778.

CHR. CRUSO   [seal]

## Sharpsburgh Hundred.

| | | | | | |
|---|---|---|---|---|---|
| 1 | Cohan, Levy | 31 | Hethrick, Vernon | 62 | Kiphart, John |
| 2 | Reynolds, Joseph (son of John) | 32 | Bremick, Daniel | 63 | Hybargor, Abraham |
| 3 | Walker, William | 33 | Fox, George | 64 | Brown, Edward |
| 4 | Smith, Joseph | 34 | Hyms, Andrew | 65 | Dick, Peter |
| 5 | Reynolds, John, Jr. | 35 | Marker, Michael | 66 | Meyer, Michl. Sr. |
| 6 | Kupro, Philip | 36 | Macsgemer, John | 67 | Flick, William |
| 7 | Baker, Mark | 37 | Steward, Thomas | 68 | Fitch, James |
| 8 | Wilkins, John | 38 | McColough, Samuel | 69 | Hoffman, Richard |
| 9 | Chapline, Moses | 39 | Baker, Abraham | 70 | Hill, James |
| 10 | Stewart, James | 40 | Knote, John | 71 | Tussy, Jacob |
| 11 | Smith, Lorance | 41 | Reynolds, Francis | 72 | Meyer, George |
| 12 | Shepard, Thomas | 42 | Fox, Frederick | 73 | Brown, James |
| 13 | Walter, William | 43 | Norman, James | 74 | Chapline, Jerimiah |
| 14 | Tamin, Ambroce | 44 | Neith, Thomas | 75 | Meyer, Peter |
| 15 | Ewart, James | 45 | Lingenfelter, Abraham | 76 | Pofsenbarger, John |
| 16 | Widmyer, William | 46 | Ham, Peter | 77 | Rockenback, Jacob |
| 17 | Nervill, William, Jr. | 47 | Meyer, Lodowick | 78 | Meyer, Jacob |
| 18 | Nervill, Joseph | 48 | Wilson, Walter | 79 | Meyer, Adam |
| 19 | Bradford, William | 49 | Hybargor, Conarod | 80 | Piper, Jacob (farmer) |
| 20 | Jackson, Hugh | 50 | Kifer, George | 81 | Kretoor, Leonard |
| 21 | Kuhno, Frederick | 51 | Hill, Peter | 82 | Pofsenbargor, Valentine |
| 22 | Read, William | 52 | Kuhns, Mathias | 83 | Hershman, Phillip |
| 23 | Peek, George | 53 | Smith, George | 84 | Flick, Adam |
| 24 | Guselor, Phillip | 54 | Helfenstone, Nicholas | 85 | Millor, David |
| 25 | Spang, Leonard | 55 | Deal, Philip | 86 | Sandman, Jacob |
| 26 | Waggoner, Phillip | 56 | Deal, George | 87 | Hyms, John |
| 27 | McKoy, Thomas | 57 | Power, Edward | 88 | Wise, Peter |
| 28 | Shop, Jacob | 58 | Spangler, Mathew | 89 | Stridor, Kilian |
| 29 | Bohrer, George | 59 | Batos, Philip | 90 | Yeats, John |
| 30 | Chapline, James | 60 | Beall, Basil | | |
| | | 61 | Sam, Nicholas | | |

## Lower Antetom Hundred.

| | | | | | |
|---|---|---|---|---|---|
| 1 | Serlott, Nicholas | 14 | Teter, Jacob | 27 | Schloser, Henry |
| 2 | Bargman, Jacob | 15 | Kurts, Christopher, Jr. | 28 | Waters, George |
| 3 | Mack, Jacob | 16 | Nichells, John | 29 | Musgraves, Henry |
| 4 | Nichodamus, Conarad | 17 | Worley, Francis | 30 | Brunner, John |
| 5 | Bargman, Frederick | 18 | Turner, James | 31 | James, Grifet |
| 6 | Knockel, Frederick | 19 | Ross, David | 32 | Mogemer, Lodowick |
| 7 | Sholly, Adam | 20 | Moonehead, Joseph | 33 | Gladhill, William |
| 8 | Hethrick, John | 21 | Billmyer, Leonard | 34 | Grunt, Adam |
| 9 | Karns, John | 22 | Sylaser, Michael | 35 | Allen, James |
| 10 | Patrick, William | 23 | Miller, Christian | 36 | Midolealf, John |
| 11 | Odonel, John | 24 | Loker, Peter | 37 | Loin, Martin |
| 12 | Shally, Peter | 25 | Loker, Michael | 38 | Placker, Samuel |
| 13 | Bucker, Phillip | 26 | Kimbol, William | | |

I do Certify that those below mentioned has solemnly, Sincerely, truely and affirm to the Oaths above mentioned. Before me

CHR. CRUSO.

## The Worshipfull Richard Davis' Returns.

| | | | | | |
|---|---|---|---|---|---|
| 1 | Williams, Basil | 17 | Shonecey, Edward | 33 | Selby, William |
| 2 | Barns, John | 18 | Fuleconar, Alexander | 34 | Hains, Joseph |
| 3 | Kendell, William | 19 | South, Thomas | 35 | Kelly, Daniel |
| 4 | Williams, Zadock | 20 | Carter, Richard | 36 | Farmer, Henry |
| 5 | Lackland, Elisha | 21 | Helame, Joseph | 37 | McLain, John |
| 6 | Simmons, Jonathan | 22 | Melott, Joseph | 38 | Ridgeley, Isaac |
| 7 | Hays, Wm. | 23 | Clark, Joseph | 39 | Roby, Michael |
| 8 | Spiers, Jeremiah | 24 | Clark, William | 40 | Phelps, John, Jr. |
| 9 | Barns, Joshua | 25 | Prather, Thomas | 41 | Jeams, Richard |
| 10 | Jacobs, Jeremiah | 26 | Davis, Amos | 42 | Barns, Nathan |
| 11 | Fonter, John | 27 | Woodhouse, David | 43 | Edmondson, Archibald |
| 12 | Lacklen, Jeremiah | 28 | Chrislie, James | 44 | Gaither, Edward, Sr. |
| 13 | Howard, Henry | 29 | Phelps, John, Sr. | 45 | Gaither, John |
| 14 | Wade, John | 30 | Moore, George | 46 | Luckett, James |
| 15 | Davis, Dennis | 31 | Brand, James | 47 | Luckett, Thomas Huz. |
| 16 | Davis, Darius | 32 | McLain, James | 48 | Corman, Daniel |

| | | | | | | | |
|---|---|---|---|---|---|---|---|
| 49 | Brand, James, Jr. | 101 | Prigmore, Jonathan | 151 | Bower, Frederick |
| 50 | Carter, Thomas | 102 | Malott, Thomas | 152 | Bateman, John |
| 51 | Simmons, Levy | 103 | Hobbins, Moses | 153 | Sallerday, Frederick |
| 52 | Griffiths, David | 104 | Higgs, James | 154 | Sallerday, John |
| 53 | Grant, John | 105 | Johnston, Thomas | 155 | Rhodes, William |
| 54 | Davis, George | 106 | South, Benjamin | 156 | Baker, Morris |
| 55 | McGlocklin, Charles | 107 | Wheat, Zadock | 157 | Baker, Benjamin |
| 56 | Jack, Jeremiah | 108 | Peter, Michael | 158 | Roby, Benjamin |
| 57 | Bowman, Sterling | 109 | Roby, William | 159 | Baker, Neshach |
| 58 | Bowman, Daniel | 110 | Tompson, William | 160 | Heaster, Nicholas |
| 59 | Sims, Richard | 111 | Barns, Ezekiah | 161 | Sallerday, Phillip |
| 60 | Jack, John | 112 | Mackinly, Patrick | 162 | Hugget, Thomas |
| 61 | Guthrie, John | 113 | Swearingen, Samuel | 163 | Estell, Daniel |
| 62 | Smith, John | 114 | Farrel, Thomas | 164 | Roby, Owen |
| 63 | Mahoney, Henry | 115 | Peddicort, Nathan | 165 | Cline, Phillip, Jr. |
| 64 | Williams, Shadrach | 116 | Pottinger, John | 166 | Berry, Bassel |
| 65 | Williams, Laurence | 117 | Molett, John | 167 | Edmonston, Nathan |
| 66 | Willson, John Enness | 118 | Sprigg, Samuel | 168 | McKinley, Archibald |
| 67 | Miller, William | 119 | Hiatt, Elisha | 169 | Dorsey, Leakin |
| 68 | Davis, Richard, Jr. | 120 | Lemaster, Hugh | 170 | Emmerson, Thomas |
| 69 | Ward, Henry | 121 | Roby, Lawrance | 171 | Spankan, Edward |
| 70 | Benwick, William | 122 | Barns, Peter | 172 | Scott, James |
| 71 | Lewis, John | 123 | Barns, Lilrannius | 173 | Baker, Zebadiah |
| 72 | Ketcham, Daniel | 124 | Barnes, Ezekiel | 174 | Baker, John Dorsey |
| 73 | Medcalf, William | 125 | Miers, George, Jr. | 175 | Bosse, David |
| 74 | Wentre, George | 126 | Barnhart, George | 176 | Rennolds, Jeremiah |
| 75 | Skeles, Ephraim | 127 | Jeames, Richard, Jr. | 177 | Lockland, Aaron |
| 76 | Skeles, William | 128 | Waters, Joseph | 178 | Shetler, William |
| 77 | Ash, Henry | 129 | Barns, Henry | 179 | Carrico, John |
| 78 | Lancy, Jeremiah | 130 | Doyle, James | 180 | Jemes, Abraham, Jr. |
| 79 | Miller, John Solomon | 131 | Barns, Joshua, son of James | 181 | Doyle, Simon |
| 80 | Skeles, Ephraim, Jr. | | | 182 | Luckett, Samuel |
| 81 | Kendall, William, Jr. | 132 | Barns, Able | 183 | Melot, Benjamin |
| 82 | Crowley, William | 133 | Barns, Joshua, son of Henry | 184 | Wheat, Joseph |
| 83 | Farmer, Samuel | | | 185 | Barns, Henry |
| 84 | Owen, Thomas | 134 | Hoyne, John | 186 | Peddicoart, Nathan |
| 85 | Stower, Michael | 135 | Wells, Jeremiah | 187 | Weele, George |
| 86 | Brown, John | 136 | Hayns, John | 188 | Gilaspy, Francis |
| 87 | Roby, Thomas | 137 | Jupin, John | 189 | Hains, Michael |
| 88 | Howard, Clement | 138 | Hepworth, John | 190 | Cline, Phillip |
| 89 | Bright, George | 139 | Swaringen, Van | 191 | Burgess, James |
| 90 | Semms, Ignatius | 140 | Belt, Benoni | 192 | Proheth, William |
| 91 | Gaither, Vechal | 141 | Housholder, Adam | 193 | Smith, James |
| 92 | Gilpin, Francis Green | 142 | Miller, John | 194 | Smith, Thomas |
| 93 | Hoskins, Joseph | 143 | Herald, Michael | 195 | Grove, John |
| 94 | Murphy, Michael | 144 | Ervin, James | 196 | Grove, Jacob |
| 95 | Smith, Robert | 145 | Crites, George | 197 | Williams, Jarrot |
| 96 | Scofield, John | 146 | Messersmith, Andrew | 198 | Shehan, William |
| 97 | Molett, Peter | 147 | Moore, John | 199 | Campbell, Robert |
| 98 | Prigmore, Theodores, Sr. | 148 | Webster, Mathias | 200 | Koogle, John |
| 99 | Prigmore, Theodores, Jr. | 149 | Baker, Gabriel | 201 | Frants, Stofel |
| 100 | Motett, Theodores | 150 | Coffer, William | 202 | Frisel, Jacob |

The afore mentioned Persons took the Oath of Fidelity before me.

RICHARD DAVIS.

## The Worshipfull Joseph Chaplin's Returns, 17 Apr., 1779.

| | | | | | |
|---|---|---|---|---|---|
| 1 | Norris, Joseph | 13 | Ekill, Harmon | 25 | Walter, Jacob |
| 2 | Smith, Phillip | 14 | Ornduff, Christopher | 26 | McNutt, Barnett |
| 3 | Norris, John | 15 | Flick, John | 27 | Mahoney, Thomas |
| 4 | McCoy, James, Sr. | 16 | Martin, James | 28 | Grove, David |
| 5 | Jackson, David | 17 | Roberts, Wm. | 29 | Motes, Davault |
| 6 | White, Peter | 18 | McCoy, John | 30 | McNutt, Alexander, Sr. |
| 7 | Orendoff, Christian | 19 | McNutt, Robert | 31 | McNutt, James |
| 8 | Cramphin, Thomas | 20 | Gardinour, Jacob | 32 | Grove, John |
| 9 | Cramphin, Ozias | 21 | Morison, Joseph | 33 | Ekill, Henry |
| 10 | Rennolds, Joseph | 22 | Conestrick, Frederick | 34 | Shanton, Ramon |
| 11 | Hogg, Thomas | 23 | McNutt, Alexander, Jr. | 35 | Furguson, John, Sr. |
| 12 | Dunkan, John | 24 | Michael, Ludwick | 36 | Reynolds, John, Sr. |

JOSEPH CHAPLIN

### The Worshipfull John Collars' Returns.

| | | | | | |
|---|---|---|---|---|---|
| 1 | Woulgemot, David | 20 | Graybail, Peter | 38 | Hartman, Adam |
| 2 | Pallmon, Peter | 21 | Hower, Anthony | 39 | Workman, John |
| 3 | Piper, Leonard | 22 | Peter, Baltksor | 40 | McLaughlin, John |
| 4 | Olinger, Philip | 23 | Olinger, Eustatious | 41 | Tomlinson, Benjn. |
| 5 | Hower, Jacob | 24 | Ridenour, Jacob | 42 | Rutter, Thomas |
| 6 | Newman, John | 25 | Acker, Casper | 43 | Simerman, Joest |
| 7 | Troseel, George | 26 | Potterof, Casper | 44 | Young, Samuel |
| 8 | Young, Michael | 27 | Ridenour, Ludwick | 45 | Smith, Nicholas |
| 9 | Kershnor, John | 28 | McLaughlip, James | 46 | Dormine, Michel |
| 10 | Poens, David | 29 | Vansweringin, Thos. | 47 | Cellar, George |
| 11 | Statlen, John | 30 | Welabergen, Matthias | 48 | Crafort, John |
| 12 | Michel, John Everhart | 31 | Faut, Banet | 49 | Bowen, Charles |
| 13 | Rutter, Abraham | 32 | Meek, David | 50 | Bowen, Frederick |
| 14 | Dice, Henry | 33 | Gabral, John | 51 | Fight, John |
| 15 | Rutter, Conrad | 34 | Boyd, William | 52 | Miller, Jacob |
| 16 | Eateniron, Martin | 35 | Boyd, Walter | 53 | Miller, Daniel |
| 17 | Smith, Daniel | 36 | Lewis, Even | 54 | Miller, Conrad |
| 18 | Kershnor, George | 37 | Sholley, Lake | 55 | Bughman, George |
| 19 | Kershnor, Jacob | | | | |

This is to certify that the within List is a true copy of my original Book of those that took the Oath of Fidelity to the State of Maryland before me.

JOHN COLLARS.

### The Worshipfull Andw. Bruce's Returns.

| | | | | | |
|---|---|---|---|---|---|
| 1 | Barritt, Lemuel | 28 | Luman, Joshua | 55 | McLoney, Alexander |
| 2 | Logsdon, William | 29 | Luman, Barton | 56 | Salmon, Christopher |
| 3 | Durbin, John | 30 | Mackenzie, Samuel | 57 | Cardry, Thomas |
| 4 | Guest, James | 31 | Tarwalter, Jacob | 58 | Harden, Larin |
| 5 | Warring, Thomas | 32 | Woolback, Adam | 59 | Salmon, Daniel |
| 6 | Nicholas, Joseph | 33 | Schultz, Jacob | 60 | Hanes, John |
| 7 | Kelly, George | 34 | Clinton, Charles | 61 | Woolback, Godfrey |
| 8 | Davison, Lewis | 35 | Humphry, Thomas | 62 | Constable, John |
| 9 | Mattingly, Richard | 36 | Durbin, Nicholas | 63 | Luman, John |
| 10 | Davis, Joshua | 37 | Mackenzie, Daniel | 64 | Luman, Moses |
| 11 | Mattingly, Joseph | 38 | Porter, Henry | 65 | Lemaster, Isaac |
| 12 | Chinoth, Richard | 39 | Carter, Denis | 66 | Mattingly, Henry |
| 13 | Tomlinson, John | 40 | Trotter, Loudon | 67 | Barkshire, "Johnse" |
| 14 | Gregg, Robert | 41 | Coulson, Charles | 68 | Chinoth, Thomas |
| 15 | Glasner, John | 42 | Leane, Henry | 69 | Ward, Edward |
| 16 | Davis, Samuel | 43 | Lazier, Joseph | 70 | Plummer, John |
| 17 | Durbin, Edward | 44 | Lazier, John | 71 | Due, Andrew |
| 18 | Mackenzie, Gabriel | 45 | Plummer, Thomas | 72 | Luman, Caleb |
| 19 | Mackenzie, Aaron | 46 | Rice, Andrew | 73 | House, Andrew |
| 20 | Richardson, George | 47 | Hill, James | 74 | Wilson, Edward |
| 21 | Nichole, John | 48 | Valentine, Frederick | 75 | Winfield, William |
| 22 | Constable, Stephen | 49 | Durbin, William | 76 | Workman, Joseph |
| 23 | Constable, Thomas | 50 | Aller, George | 77 | Workman, Stephen |
| 24 | Mattingly, Barnet | 51 | Haagland, James | 78 | Workman, Andrew |
| 25 | Simpkins, Dickinson | 52 | Durbin, Samuel | 79 | Workman, John |
| 26 | Swank, David | 53 | Kennedy, John | 80 | Workman, Isaac |
| 27 | Simpkins, Dickenson, Sr. | 54 | Connar, Timothy | 81 | Marsner, Joseph |

Washington County, 2d Mch., 1778. I Certify to the Honorable the Governor and Council, that the within persons gave their affirmation to and subscribed the Oath of Fidelity to the State of Maryland according to the Act of Assembly and that this is a true Copy of the Book kept by me for that purpose and delivered to the Clerk of this County as ordered.

ANDW. BRUCE.

## 1 *The Worshipfull Samuel Barrits' Returns.*

| | | | | | |
|---|---|---|---|---|---|
| 2 | Cresop, Daniel | 55 | Maichal, John | 109 | Stratford, Joshua |
| 3 | Cresop, Joseph | 56 | Clark, Richard | 110 | Staddert, James—Feb. 25. |
| 4 | Gunterman, Henry | 57 | Dial, Tarance | 111 | Cresop, Thomas |
| 5 | Ranady, John | 58 | Gunteman, Peter | 112 | Conrad, Henry |
| 6 | Dorson, William, Sr. | 59 | Gragg, Robert, Jr. | 113 | Kimberlin, John |
| 7 | Dewitt, Martin | 60 | Ayers, Moses, Sr. | 114 | Power, Benjamin |
| 8 | Kimbelan, Jacob | 61 | Dawson, Edward | 115 | Clark, Jonathan |
| 9 | Rashr, William | 62 | Lee, Joseph | 116 | Grimes, William |
| 10 | Anderson, William | 63 | Dewitt, Peter | 117 | Reed, Joseph |
| 11 | Dorson, Edward | 64 | Davies, Joseph | 118 | Talbard, Thomas |
| 12 | Hubbs, Samuel | 65 | Roman, Reynon | 119 | Crage, James |
| 13 | Callard, Joseph | 66 | Dawson, Thomas | 120 | Parker, Nathaniel |
| 14 | Ritchards, Geo. Hall | 67 | Layport, George | 121 | Prather, James. |
| 15 | Quick, Dennis | 68 | Dorson, Allon | 122 | Scott, John |
| 16 | Quick, Thomas | 69 | Dorson, Edward | 123 | Posttethwort, William |
| 17 | Quick, Jacob | 70 | King, John | 124 | Allin, Jeremiah |
| 18 | Quick, Aaron | 71 | Right, Samuel | 125 | Clark, John |
| 19 | Munop, Moses | 72 | Thornin, Alworth | 126 | Horn, Vallentine |
| 20 | Quick, Andrew | 73 | Ball, Zapheniah | 127 | Clouge, William |
| 21 | Quick, Benjamin | 74 | Hull, Benjamin | 128 | Russell, Callob |
| 22 | Bonham, Peter | 75 | Lee, Joseph, Jr. | 129 | Cassart, William |
| 23 | Breeze, Andrew | 76 | Anderson, Jeremiah | 130 | Pairs, James |
| 24 | Lee, Wm.—Jan. 27, 1778 | 77 | Oldwort, Jacob | 131 | Cassart, Daniel |
| 25 | Dorson, James, Jr. | 78 | Mounts, Joseph | 132 | Barsman, John |
| 26 | Martin, Nehemiah | 79 | Lethworth, Lanord | 133 | Flock, Jacob |
| 27 | Dorson, James, Sr. | 80 | Heaton, Michel | 134 | Lapear, William |
| 28 | Lindsey, John, Sr. | 81 | Ranaday, Charles | 135 | Pursel, Daniel |
| 29 | Little, Peter | 82 | Coman, John | 136 | Pursel, Thomas |
| 30 | Bray, Henry | 83 | Coy, John | 137 | Bsnedker, Crosteon |
| 31 | Quick, Aaron, Jr. | 84 | Devitt, Henry | | (Snedker?) |
| 32 | Lovitt, Daniel | 85 | Fethworth, Isaac | 138 | Pursel, John |
| 33 | Lovitt, Britton | 86 | Ray, William | 139 | Focpeh, George |
| 34 | Crow, Philip | 87 | Markwell, George | 140 | Ward, Edward |
| 35 | Laycock, Isaac—5 Feb., 1778. | 88 | Swan, George | 141 | Bell, John |
| 36 | Forgerson, Samuel | 89 | Gunerman, Henry, Jr. | 142 | Hartely, Homes |
| 37 | Munroe, Robert | 90 | Inslow, Joseph | 143 | Hartely, John |
| 38 | Feaild, Thomas | 91 | Blew, Abraham | 144 | Collyer, Isaac, Jr. |
| 39 | Culver, Jonathan | 92 | Smith, David | 145 | Collyer, Isaac, Sr. |
| 40 | Williams, James | 93 | Atheron, Aaron, Jr. | 146 | Chinorsath, Thomas |
| 41 | Ogle, William | 94 | Lee, Samuel | 147 | Charrey, Thomas |
| 42 | Rook, Thos. James | 95 | House, John | 148 | Been, John |
| 43 | Ward, Cosnealve | 96 | Hirsh, John | 149 | Smith, James |
| 44 | Cresop, Daniel, Jr. | 97 | Coy, John, Jr. | 150 | Lindsey, John, Sr. |
| 45 | Atherton, Aaron | 98 | Dewitt, James | 151 | Crow, Philip |
| 46 | Atherton, Joshua | 99 | Gordon, William | 152 | Claxton, Samuel |
| 47 | Atherton, Benjamin | 100 | Wintors, James | 153 | Johnson, Benj., Snr., of |
| 48 | Dumeagin, Roger | 101 | Petters, Abraham | | Wm. Johnson |
| 49 | Dewitt, Barney | 102 | Prather, Charles | 154 | Hubart, John |
| 50 | Tracy, Timothy | 103 | Johnson, William | 155 | Willerson, Jeremiah |
| 51 | Hughnns, Aaron | 104 | Fower, James | 156 | Hugham, Moses |
| 52 | James, Eran | 105 | Wiggins, Philip | 157 | Pursell, David |
| 53 | Ayers, Moses, Jr. | 106 | Flower, Robert | 158 | Howell, William |
| 54 | Atherton, John | 107 | Tramell, Philip | 159 | Deware, Isaac |
| | | 108 | Moore, William | 160 | Logston, Isaac |

I certify that this is a true Copy.

16 Mch., 1778.                              SAMUEL BARRITS.

## 1 *The Worshipfull John Barnes' Returns.*

| | | | | | |
|---|---|---|---|---|---|
| 2 | Gillespie, George | 12 | McFall, John | 22 | Gillespie, Thomas |
| 3 | Songue, John | 13 | Campbell, Francis | 23 | Ankeny, John |
| 4 | Oharra, Patrick | 14 | Bean, John | 24 | Gerlock, Henry |
| 5 | Gall, George | 15 | Miller, Adam | 25 | Bonnett, John |
| 6 | Replogh, Philop | 16 | Rough, George | 26 | Fiery, Joseph |
| 7 | Baker, Isaac | 17 | Rough, Peter | 27 | Prather, Richard |
| 8 | Killogh, Allen | 18 | Moore, Philip | 28 | Bruir, Joseph |
| 9 | Edmonson, Thomas | 19 | Painter, Godfrey | 29 | Gilbert, John |
| 10 | McFall, Neal | 20 | Paule, James | 30 | Reips, John |
| 11 | Campbell, Daniel | 21 | Ankeny, Levolt | 31 | Woth, Christopher |

| | | | | | |
|---|---|---|---|---|---|
| 32 | Bruir, Peter | 64 | Beven, Leonard | 96 | Boughslough, Peter |
| 33 | Tesern, Frederick | 65 | Welch, William | 97 | Craig, Philip |
| 34 | Bouttauff, Andrew | 66 | Hughes, James | 98 | Trumpower, Leonard |
| 35 | Seibert, Jacob | 67 | Kiernan, Michael | 99 | Moore, Christopher |
| 36 | Bouttauff, Martin | 68 | Heatherrington, John | 100 | Caput, John |
| 37 | Cline, John | 69 | Augustus, Joseph | 101 | Hopponhiger, John |
| 38 | Fisher, Adam | 70 | Moore, Joseph | 102 | Shaver, George |
| 39 | Davis, John Barton | 71 | Carlock, Adam | 103 | Shaver, Powell |
| 40 | McMackin, Thomas | 72 | Chrossen, John | 104 | Seigeart, John |
| 41 | Pry, John | 73 | Know, John | 105 | McMackin, Banaby |
| 42 | Sistwoort, Valentine | 74 | Rough, John | 106 | Strong, James |
| 43 | Erth, Christopher | 75 | Easter, George | 107 | Malcome, James |
| 44 | Beard, David | 76 | Worth, Peter | 108 | Kelly, Patrick |
| 45 | Nesbett, Nathaniel | 77 | Stoll, Henry | 109 | Mathews, William |
| 46 | Peck, George | 78 | Easter, Peter | 110 | Snyder, John |
| 47 | Adam, William | 79 | McClain, James | 111 | Sparling, Andrew |
| 48 | Foard, Robert | 80 | Mugg, Thomas | 112 | Rouff, Nicholas |
| 49 | Foard, Henry | 81 | Worley, Thomas | 113 | Carn, Philip |
| 50 | Williams, Joseph | 82 | McCullam, Alexander | 114 | Taylor, John |
| 51 | Prather, Basil | 83 | Millhouse, John | 115 | Downy, Richard |
| 52 | Winsen, Richard | 84 | McKinnan, Michael | 116 | Shaver, Peter |
| 53 | Wolgomot, Joseph | 85 | Morford, Daniel | 117 | Clark, Francis |
| 54 | Snyder, Anthony | 86 | Rerls, Frederick | 118 | Thompson, Joseph |
| 55 | Prather, Thomas | 87 | Cow, Henry | 119 | Read, Samuel |
| 56 | Blackmore, William | 88 | Ward, Jacob | 120 | Mayes, Andrew |
| 57 | Foard, James | 89 | Raughly, George | 121 | Burk, John |
| 58 | Welsh, William | 90 | Charlton, Thomas | 122 | Jarques, Thomas |
| 59 | Shule, William | 91 | Hill, William | 123 | Kennedy, David |
| 60 | James, George | 92 | Claircomb, Henry | 124 | Bachus, Benjamin |
| 61 | Huth, Richard | 93 | Fivecoats, Michael | 125 | Fear, George |
| 62 | Blackmore, Calep | 94 | Sibert, Jacob | | |
| 63 | McCollam, Thomas | 95 | Nevil, George | | |

Sworn before me.

WASHINGTON COUNTY, Feb. 28, 1778.

JOHN BARNES.

*The Worshipfull John Stull's Returns.*

| | | | | | |
|---|---|---|---|---|---|
| 1 | Asher, Gabril | 32 | Conrad, John | 63 | Hersman, Andrew |
| 2 | Bower, Morris | 33 | Cooper, Isaac | 64 | Hersman, Mathias |
| 3 | Brooke, Thomas | 34 | Clagett, Bothumas | 65 | Hogmire, Conrad |
| 4 | Blume, Henry | 35 | Cline, Joseph | 66 | Hoover, Christopher |
| 5 | Bower, George | 36 | Custore, George | 67 | Henry, Nicholas |
| 6 | Baker, Bastin | 37 | Creal, William | 68 | Heaiskill, Benjamin |
| 7 | Barnhend, George | 38 | Darling, Lott | 69 | Johnson, Barney |
| 8 | Botts, Andrew | 39 | Drake, Joseph | 70 | Jacoby, Conrad |
| 9 | Brendlinges, Conrad | 40 | Davis, Robert | 71 | Kirkpatrick, William |
| 10 | Barns, Uz. | 41 | Diuerling, John | 72 | Kreuger, Peter |
| 11 | Blacher, Frederick | 42 | Earley, Abram | 73 | Kelly, William |
| 12 | Baker, William | 43 | Fair, Francis | 74 | Karshnor, Martin |
| 13 | Bilmore, John | 44 | Forgresong, Christian | 75 | Kaler, Frederick |
| 14 | Bungarnor, Jacob | 45 | Fitch, Joseph | 76 | Kaler, Daniel |
| 15 | Bell, Charles | 46 | Fage, John | 77 | Klosner, George |
| 16 | Boond, John | 47 | Frend, "Cacob" | 78 | Klapper, Wallingtine |
| 17 | Burges, Francis | 48 | Fye, William | 79 | Klapper, Harmen |
| 18 | Baur, Michael | 49 | Filman, Mathias | 80 | Kirkpatrick, Michael |
| 19 | Baker, Peter | 50 | Gunity, William | 81 | Kirkpatrick, James |
| 20 | Bergd, Peter | 51 | Gable, Phillips | 82 | Lizer, Mathias |
| 21 | Baum, Bartolome | 52 | Gyer, John | 83 | Litherman, Michael |
| 22 | Beresford, John | 53 | Gyer, Frederick | 84 | Lidac, Michael |
| 23 | Besty, Wm. | 54 | Gyer, Frederick | 85 | Lorry, Henry |
| 24 | Commina, Wm. | 55 | Gairing, Christopher | 86 | Livingstone, John |
| 25 | Commins, William | 56 | Gellespe, David | 87 | Louele, Thomas |
| 26 | Claubough, Martin | 57 | Gardner, Francis | 88 | Messersmith, Wallintine |
| 27 | Duse, Christopher | 58 | Gray, Robert | 89 | Mock, Peter |
| 28 | Craturn, Robert | 59 | Housholler, Jacob | 90 | Miller, Ulrick |
| 29 | Commins, John | 60 | Hofman, Michael | 91 | Miller, Solomon |
| 30 | Conrad, Daniel | 61 | Howard, John | 92 | Martain, Robert |
| 31 | Conrad, John | 62 | Hewett, Christopher | 93 | Mengennor, John |

| | | |
|---|---|---|
| 94 Moffet, William | 118 Swank, John | 141 Shailer, Michael |
| 95 Miller, Frederick | 119 Smith, John | 142 Shailer, Peter |
| 96 Miller, George | 120 Shilling, Phillip | 143 Shock, Frederick |
| 97 McCollough, William | 121 Sharer, Peter | 144 Swingley, Leonard |
| 98 McCoy, Archabald | 122 Sibird, John | 145 Sookey, Martain |
| 99 Miller, John | 123 Sibird, Peter | 146 Staler, William |
| 100 Nichols, Isaac | 124 Swingly, George | 147 Space, Daniel |
| 101 Nageley, Peter | 125 Swingley, Michael | 148 Elie, William |
| 102 Ox, William | 126 Swingly, George | 149 Walker, John |
| 103 Paul, William | 127 Syster, Daniel | 150 Winder, James |
| 104 Prue, Joseph | 128 Syster, Michael | 151 Winder, Jacob |
| 105 Pence, Jacob | 129 Snider, Henry | 152 Winder, Daniel |
| 106 Rutter, Edward | 130 Smith, Jacob | 153 Wikel, Henry |
| 107 Rutter, John | 131 Smith, John | 154 Wollinger, Wollentine |
| 108 Rutter, Alexander | 132 Smith, David | 155 Winder, Thomas |
| 109 Rutter, William | 133 Snider, Frederick | 156 Wessa, Jacob |
| 110 Rutter, Edmond | 134 Swingly, Nicholas | 157 Winder, James |
| 111 Refneh, Casper | 135 Shaver, John | 158 Wiles, William |
| 112 Swearingen, Charles | 136 Star, William | 159 Whitstone, Bolser |
| 113 Sharer, George | 137 Snider, Martin | 160 Waggoner, Peter |
| 114 Sharer, Isaac | 138 Strider, Philip | 161 Yost, Henry |
| 115 Sharer, Jacob | 139 Shank, Peter | 162 Gilhart, Christopher |
| 116 Smith, George | 140 Shank, Peter | 163 Zachariah, Jacob |
| 117 Swank, Jacob | | |

A true Copy of persons who have taken the Oaths of Fidelity before

### JOHN STULL.

### *The Worshipfull William Yates' Returns.*

| | | |
|---|---|---|
| 1 Allen, John | 29 Gillispye, John | 57 Millme, John |
| 2 Acton, Richard | 30 George, Samuel | 58 Noyse, Thomas |
| 3 Allum, Thomas | 31 Gilbert, Michael | 59 Otto, Matthias |
| 4 Anderson, Charles | 32 Garlock, John | 60 Phillips, Thomas |
| 5 Barnhart, George | 33 Herron, John | 61 Pearce, Benjamin |
| 6 Bryson, Archibald | 34 Hynes, William | 62 Postle, Samuel |
| 7 Byrne, Michael | 35 Hynes, Thomas | 63 Pindle, Jacob |
| 8 Beane, Henry | 36 Howard, Philip | 64 Potts, Jonathan |
| 9 Beane, John | 37 Harrison, John | 65 Potts, Samuel |
| 10 Black, John | 38 Harrison, William | 66 Pitcach, Benjamin |
| 11 Burroughs, John | 39 Harrison, James | 67 Rickold, Maynard |
| 12 Chattwell, Thomas | 40 Hale, Joseph | 68 Rose, Jonathan |
| 13 Campbell, George | 41 Jinkison, Matthew | 69 Reed, Richard |
| 14 Cummings, Juba | 42 Johnson, William | 70 Smithson, Daniel |
| 15 Cox, Abram | 43 Jacobs, Gabrial | 71 Stillwell, Jeremiah |
| 16 Cox, Isaac | 44 Jones, Samuel | 72 Sands, Thomas |
| 17 Cox, Jacob | 45 Johnson, Benjamin | 73 Swails, William |
| 18 Clarck, John | 46 King, John | 74 Snyder, Adam |
| 19 Clarck, Robert | 47 Little, Jessa | 75 Snyder, Peter |
| 20 Clarck, Bazil | 48 Lynn, John | 76 Skinner, William |
| 21 Clarck, John | 49 Myers, Elias | 77 Smith, Jachabod |
| 22 Dunnavan, Daniel | 50 Martin, William | 78 Wiggons, William |
| 23 Daugharty, William | 51 McHeil, John | 79 Wiggons, Uriah |
| 24 Draydon, James | 52 Mills, Jacob | 80 Walch, William |
| 25 Flint, Joseph | 53 Mills, James | 81 Walls, Hathan |
| 26 Flint, John | 54 Martin, Joseph | 82 Webb, John |
| 27 Flora, John | 55 Martin, William, Jr. | 83 Wiggons, John |
| 28 Flora, James | 56 Mount, John | |

The names of the People that have taken the Oath of Fidelity in Obedience to an Act of Assembly by living in Linton and Frederick Hundreds in the County of Washington.

### WILLIAM YATES.

## The Worshipfull Henry Schnebely's Returns.

| | | | | | | | |
|---|---|---|---|---|---|---|---|
| 1 | Woltz, George | 71 | Keibler, George | 141 | Smith, Joseph |
| 2 | Woltz, Peter | 72 | Jones, Thomas | 142 | Jerkel, George |
| 3 | Zott, Michael | 73 | Leidy, Adam | 143 | Olinger, Jacob |
| 4 | Peifer, Martin | 74 | Fisher, Daniel | 144 | Brather, Rignal |
| 5 | Hraber, Jacob | 75 | Rouff, Mathias | 145 | Shneider, Casper |
| 6 | Branner, Philip | 76 | Aspey, Jacob | 146 | Kaufman, Adam |
| 7 | Ragan, John | 77 | Young, Revd. George | 147 | Shneider, Daniel |
| 8 | Forster, Luke | 78 | Adam, John, Jr. | 148 | Miller, George |
| 9 | Shryach, Leonard | 79 | Hagger, John | 149 | Coone, David |
| 10 | Shryach, John | 80 | Adam, Peter | 150 | Bumgartner, Adam |
| 11 | Hendrick, Charles | 81 | Patterson, James | 151 | Keissinger, George |
| 12 | Nead, Mathias | 82 | Miller, Hans | 152 | Keitzmiller, Casper |
| 13 | Young, Ludwig | 83 | Feigety, Peter | 153 | Nihy, George |
| 14 | Reitenower, Henry | 84 | Troxal, Abraham | 154 | Groff, Jacob |
| 15 | Hix, Jacob | 85 | Bowman, Jacob | 155 | Rapp, Matthias |
| 16 | Ott, Jacob | 86 | Reichel, Adam | 156 | Wattstein, John |
| 17 | Hook, Peter | 87 | Guthere, Robert | 157 | Thomas, Jacob |
| 18 | Bowman, John | 88 | Pflenger, Leonard | 158 | Raymer, John |
| 19 | Hower, Anthony | 89 | Krombach, John | 159 | Stettwell, Stephen |
| 20 | Bowman, Aron | 90 | Bowen, Frederick | 160 | Burn, Christian |
| 21 | Kirshner, David | 91 | Kerenenkan, Ludwig | 161 | Whiteman, Jacob |
| 22 | Stampel, Godfries | 92 | Wullenshleger, Jacob | 162 | Schwengel, Nicholas |
| 23 | Schnegenberger, Christian | 93 | Wagner, John | 163 | Nigh, George |
| 24 | Edelman, Adam | 94 | Conner, William | 164 | Houshatter, John |
| 25 | Jones, David, Jr. | 95 | Slack, Martin | 165 | Mower, Nicholas |
| 26 | Black, Samuel | 96 | Lower, Michael | 166 | Guntryman, Henry |
| 27 | Black, Wm. | 97 | Reinhart, George | 167 | Schwengel, George, Jr. |
| 28 | Opp, Nicholas | 98 | Donney, John | 168 | Miller, Michael |
| 29 | Flennard, John, Jr. | 99 | Brown, Conrad | 169 | Fahrman, Henry |
| 30 | Hagger, Michael | 100 | Ritter, Jacob | 170 | Wermer, Revd. Jacob |
| 31 | Miller, Henry | 101 | Ritter, Elias | 171 | Davis, John |
| 32 | Deibly, Jacob | 102 | Nicodemus, Conrad | 172 | Hentz, John |
| 33 | Seitzler, William | 103 | Skinner, Wm. | 173 | Barns, Deitrick |
| 34 | Figeby, John | 104 | Burckhart, George | 174 | Adam, Jacob |
| 35 | Startzman, Henry | 105 | Rietenower, Nicholas | 175 | Hughes, Thomas |
| 36 | Uhrenban, Jacob | 106 | Heofflick, Peter | 176 | Pine, James |
| 37 | Reitenower, Nicholas | 107 | Petry, Jacob | 177 | Albright, Peter |
| 38 | Weiss, George | 108 | Keibler, Jacob | 178 | Wyand, Joseph |
| 39 | Danner, Jacob | 109 | Soutter, Felix | 179 | Meek, Thomas |
| 40 | Nichol, Jacob | 110 | Kleine, Henry | 180 | Alder, Christopher |
| 41 | Makillip, Henry | 111 | Schultz, George | 181 | Kersseker, Simon |
| 42 | Emerick, Jonas | 112 | Hoffman, Casper | 182 | Bousser, John |
| 43 | Nadenbush, Thomas | 113 | Bordam, Jacob | 183 | Gabral, Abraham |
| 44 | Christman, Paul | 114 | Kleinsmith, Andrew | 184 | Krout, Peter |
| 45 | Ho—, A. | 115 | Schuhman, John | 185 | Kore, Christian |
| 46 | Reitenower, Henry | 116 | Kirshman, Martin | 186 | Reitenower, Matthias |
| 47 | Fruth, Martin | 117 | Reitenswer, Jacob | 187 | Heoffety, Carte |
| 48 | Rehb, John | 118 | Harry, Jonathan | 188 | Cameron, Ludwig |
| 49 | Trapp, Christian | 119 | Weiss, John George | 189 | Flennard, Rudolph |
| 50 | Bonman, Simon | 120 | Sceittner, Martin | 190 | Seller, Jacob |
| 51 | Dubilbis, Michael | 121 | Weiarich, Jacob | 191 | Schweitzer, John |
| 52 | Reitenower, David | 122 | Harry, David | 192 | Cockran, William |
| 53 | Startzman, Henry | 123 | Deil, George | 193 | Keisseker, Philip |
| 54 | Maconkey, Jacob | 124 | Young, Eustachius | 194 | Watson, James |
| 55 | Maconkey, John | 125 | Harsh, Frederick | 195 | Lorg, Nicholas |
| 56 | Hoblitzel, Adrian | 126 | Mandey, Balthasar | 196 | Miller, John |
| 57 | Werger, Leonard | 127 | Reymer, Frederick | 197 | Rickenbach, —— |
| 58 | Deitz, Ernst | 128 | Oster, Adam | 198 | Schnebely, Henry, Jr. |
| 59 | Bleny, Rudolph | 129 | Oster, Jacob | 199 | Bernth, Jacob |
| 60 | Hagger, Jonathan | 130 | Hens, Jacob | 200 | Glass, Michael |
| 61 | Rue, Isaac | 131 | Eakenberger, Michael | 201 | Reitenower, Henry, Jr. |
| 62 | Gibler, Jacob | 132 | Houshatter, Michael | 202 | Miller, Henry, son of Hans |
| 63 | Dorner, Michael | 133 | Weber, Engell | 203 | Miller, Henry, son of Conrad |
| 64 | Hess, William | 134 | Kershner, Philip | | |
| 65 | Shneider, John | 135 | Fetzer, Philip | 204 | Momonghan, John |
| 66 | Rouff, Michael | 136 | Houshatter, Gorge | 205 | Fisher, Abraham |
| 67 | Rouff, Anthony | 137 | Salter, Samuel | 206 | Bawyer, John Urick |
| 68 | Their, Michael | 138 | Care, Arthur | 207 | Konhn, George |
| 69 | Young, George | 139 | Handlen, Stephen | 208 | Young, John |
| 70 | Jones, John | 140 | Care, Francis | 209 | Thomer, Ludwig |

| | | |
|---|---|---|
| 210 Steinvauffer, John | 230 Naffe, George | 250 Barvard, Henry |
| 211 Witterich, Jacob | 231 Dussing, Philip | 251 Brackaunier, Peter |
| 212 Secttner, John Conrad | 232 Meyer, Felix | 252 Groff, Jacob, Jr. |
| 213 Mahniger, Henry | 233 Rietenower, Martin | 253 Kreehbawm, Philip |
| 214 Nagel, David | 234 Barringer, Adam | 254 Leimbach, John |
| 215 Stare, John | 235 Rietenower, George | 255 Krofft, Frederick |
| 216 Rigger, John | 236 Bower, Abraham | 256 Mooll, Henry |
| 217 Rigger, Casper | 237 Naffe, Leonard | 257 Leishser, Adam |
| 218 Harry, Martin, Jr. | 238 Brandstatter, Andrew | 258 Donney, William |
| 219 Eckenberger, Jacob | 239 Standerson, Gerard | 259 Phleuger, Peter |
| 220 Greylish, Francis | 240 Bower, Maurice | 260 House, John |
| 221 Rieffennach, Philip | 241 Poth, Michael | 261 Hartel, Michael |
| 222 Oster, Conrad | 242 Casherdy, John | 262 Fackler, Michael |
| 223 Shoffer, Dewald | 243 Lowry, Jacob | 263 Cameron, Adam |
| 224 Reihnhold, Fittus | 244 Housholder, Simon | 264 Miller, John |
| 225 Huerd, Ludwig | 245 Shutz, Conrad | 265 Schnebely, John |
| 226 Kuhns, Jacob | 246 Mowen, Daniel | 266 Snheder, John |
| 227 Bresh, Philip | 247 Sailler, Peter | 267 Zapp, George |
| 228 Gayrherd, John | 248 Schnell, Henry | 268 Shug, Jacob |
| 229 Durgler, George | 249 Sailler, John | 269 Fleunard, John |

I hereby certify that this is a true Copy from the Original List, Sworn by me.

HENRY SCHNEBELY.

A List of Such that did Afirm before me.

270 Schultz, George        271 Rictenawer, Peter

HENRY SCHNEBELY.

### The Worshipfull Andrew Rentch's Returns, 7 Mch. 1778.

| | | |
|---|---|---|
| 1 Bell, Anthony | 13 Huninger, Andrew | 24 Ridenour, Martain |
| 2 Benedict, Bowman | 14 Hinsman, Joseph | 25 Roof, Rudey |
| 3 Beala, Peter | 15 Houk, Jacob | 26 Rimill, Phillip |
| 4 Clapsadle, Daniel | 16 Karshnor, Jonathan | 27 Shriver, John |
| 5 Corrowfiow, George | 17 Lang, Thomas | 28 Shriver, Henry |
| 6 Conkry, William | 18 Lighter, Abraham | 29 Shoumaker, Balser |
| 7 Dager, Michal | 19 Lighter, Jacob | 30 Shock, Christian |
| 8 Earhart, Phillip | 20 Nicodemus, Frederick | 31 Tresal, Goodhart |
| 9 Faur, Henry | 21 Perey, Joseph | 32 Troxel, Abraham |
| 10 Grading, Isaac | 22 Pifer, Manuell | 33 Wert, Jacob |
| 11 George, Thomas | 23 Pinkley, Jacob | 34 Winder, George |
| 12 Hartle, Frederick | | |

A true List, Washington County. For the Governor and Council of Maryland.

ANDREW RENTCH'S RETURNS.

### The Worshipfull Joseph Sprigg's Returns.

| | | |
|---|---|---|
| 1 Walling, James | 17 Griem, John Adam | 33 Conrad, William |
| 2 Walling, Delashmut | 18 Diel, Adam | 34 Unsell, John |
| 3 Stidinger, Frederick | 19 Mandel, Christian | 35 Wise, Adam |
| 4 Smith, Adam | 20 Douglass, Robert | 36 Ott, Adam |
| 5 Pullen, William | 21 Douglass, Samuel | 37 Morgan, Nathaniel |
| 6 Oster, John | 22 Harvey, Martin | 38 Hieskell, Frederick |
| 7 Powell, Nathan | 23 Hawk, Peter | 39 Quinn, George |
| 8 Beatty, Mark | 24 Teachler, John | 40 Maddin, Mordica |
| 9 Waggoner, Francis | 25 Hockey, Nicholas | 41 Price, Josiah |
| 10 Fisher, Jacob | 26 Ridenowo, Matthias | 42 Douglass, William |
| 11 Rinehart, Thomas | 27 Hockey, Christopher | 43 Baker, John |
| 12 Harnidge, Philip | 28 Webb, John, Sr. | 44 Brown, William |
| 13 Beltzhoover, Melchor | 29 Webb, John, Jr. | 45 Dawney, William |
| 14 Boyd, William, Sr. | 30 Hinde, John | 46 Stewart, George |
| 15 Shryock, Herry | 31 Tutwiler, Henry | 47 Ridgely, Frederick |
| 16 Selhart, Godfrey | 32 Leidy, John | 48 Downey, Samuel |

| 49 Downey, James | 68 Reuh, Mathias | 87 Webb, William |
|---|---|---|
| 50 Downey, William (son of Jas.) | 69 Ware, Martin | 88 Mong, Adam |
| | 70 Rice, Nicholas | 89 Mong, Nicholas |
| 51 Dawney, David | 71 McFeely, Edward | 90 Scott, John |
| 52 Dilts, John | 72 Flack, James | 91 Scott, David |
| 53 Brown, George | 73 Clauner, Daniel | 92 Scott, William |
| 54 Savage, John | 74 Walford, Adam | 93 Sunon, Peter |
| 55 Sailor, Mathias | 75 Rigger, Peter | 94 Sirlott, Nicholas |
| 56 Alder, Frederick | 76 Sidenor, Frederick | 95 Reed, Samuel |
| 57 Kalehofer, Devalt | 77 Sidenor, Christopher | 96 Herburn, John |
| 58 Bower, Jacob | 78 Stortzman, John George | 97 Allison, Robert |
| 59 George, Joseph | 79 Elliott, David | 98 Downing, William |
| 60 Wetz, Jacob | 80 Householder, Adam | 99 Downirg, Joseph |
| 61 Baird, William | 81 Crauner, Ernest | 100 Gutrhale, Lodwick |
| 62 Wetztone, Peter | 82 Iclebarger, Conrad | 101 Branon, Patrick |
| 63 Bauman, Martin | 83 Kernecome, John | 102 Hore, Peter |
| 64 Keene, Daniel | 84 Stewart, James | 103 McPherrin, Thomas |
| 65 Miller, William | 85 Fisher, John | 104 Tyther, Peter |
| 66 Ultheart, Lawrence | 86 Fisher, Jacob | 105 Stare, Christian |
| 67 Lutrode, John | | |

I do hereby Certify that the persons mentioned in the aforegoing List were Qualified agreeable to the Directions of An Act of Assembly Entitled an Act for the Better Security of the Government. Given under my hand 1st day Apl., 1778.

JOS. SPRIGG.

---

## ACT OF ASSEMBLY, 5 FEBRUARY, 1777.

"At a Session of the General Assembly of Maryland, convened by the Council of Safety, and begun and held at the City of Annapolis, on Wednesday the fifth of February, in the Year of our Lord one thousand seven hundred and seventy-seven, the following Laws were enacted."

"An Act to punish certain crimes and misdemeanors, and to prevent the growth of toryism.

Chapter XX, Sec. XIII. "That every senator, delegate to congress or assembly, member of the council, electors of the senate, and every attorney at law, and all civil officers, and all persons holding any office of trust or profit in this state, shall take, repeat and subscribe the following oath of fidelity and support to this state, before he acts as such, or enters into the execution of his office, to wit: I, A. B. do swear that I do not hold myself bound to yield any allegiance or obedience to the King of Great Britain, his heirs or successors, and that I will be true and faithful to the state of Maryland, and will, to the utmost of my power, support, maintain and defend the freedom and independence thereof, and the government as now established, against all open enemies and secret and traitorous conspiracies, and will use my utmost endeavors to disclose and make known to the governor, or some one of the judges or justices thereof, all treasons of traitorous conspiracies, attempts or combinations against this state or the government thereof, which may come to my knowledge; so help me God. (See also pp. 1, 11)

Section XIV. "That every member of the present general assembly, and the council, shall take, repeat and subscribe, the said oath, immediately after the passing this Act, and before he acts as such; and if any person now holding any office of trust or profit, shall not, within three months after the end of this present session, take, repeat and subscribe, the same oath, or affirmation if a quaker, menonist or dunker, he shall be ipso facto disqualified to hold such office, and the office of such person shall be filled agreeable to its institution."

Sec. XV, "And be it enacted That every Voter for Delegates or Sheriffs, or for Electors of the Senate, if required, and every other Person required by Law to take the Oath of Fidelity and Support to this State, shall take, repeat, and subscribe the same Oath, or if a Quaker, Menonist or Dunker, shall solemnly, sincerely, and truly declare and affirm thereto in the Words thereof."

Sec. XVIII, "Provided always, that nothing herein contained shall extend to such persons who from religious principles have not subscribed or shall not subscribe the association."

Sec. XIX, "And be it enacted, That this Act shall be publicly read by the Clerk of the General Court, and by the Clerk of every County Court in this State, at their next Court respectively, immediately after impannelling the Grand Jury, and also by every Minister, Teacher or Preacher of the Gospel, immediately after divine Service, at every Church, Chapel, or Meeting-House, where they officiate, on some Sunday in the Month of May next; and every Clerk, Minister, Teacher or Preacher, failing so to do, shall forfeit and pay the Sum of five Pounds, to be recovered with Costs by the Informer before any Justice of the Peace of the County where the Offence shall be committed."

### FREDERICK COUNTY, MARYLAND, 1778

"A LIST OF PERSONS IN FREDERICK COUNTY WHO HAVE TAKEN THE FOLLOW-
ING OATH BEFORE THE DIFFERENT MAGISTRATES AS MENTIONED
BELOW; AND RETURNED BY THEM TO FREDERICK COURT."*

"Taken Before the Worshipful Justice, One Return, 337 Men, Recorded."

"A List of the names of Sundry Persons who made their appearance in Open Court, and who after giving reasons which the Court deemed satisfactory, why they did not take the Oath of Fidelity and Support to the State of Maryland, agreeable in the last Act of Assembly, by permission of the said Court did severally and respectively take and repeat agreeable to the provision in the same Act contained."

(The Oath is published on pp 1, 11.)

| | | |
|---|---|---|
| Ancrum, Richd., Sr. | Bounds, Thos. | Bayley, George |
| Ancrum, Jacob, Jr. | Berger, John | Braudsaburgh, Samuel |
| Ancrum, Richd., Jr. | Burgess, James | Bakell, Jacob |
| Angle, Jacob | Bromer, Peter | Bastain, Michl. |
| Acord, Joseph | Broomer, Henry | Beall, Ninian |
| Armse, Robert | Beatty, Wm. | Barnoser, Danl. |
| Argle, John | Burton, Henry | Barnoser, George |
| Apple, Peter | Bluebaug, Jacob | Baum, Jacob |
| Ambrose, Henry | Brook, Roger | |
| Arnold, George | Brueback, Rudolph | Carvill, John |
| | Broadback, Henry | Cater, Jas. |
| Byfield, Robert | Beckett, Wm. | Coontz, Martin |
| Belter, Peter | Beckett, James | Cecil, Philip |
| Boogher, Andro | Boone, Abrum | Cover, Argheart |
| Balsel, Peter | Beckett, Wm. | Conse, Patrick |
| Brown, George | Bayer, Jacob | Coontz, Henry |
| Rockes, John | Barkshire, Henry | Cline, Jacob |
| Beamer, Henry | Brown, Thos. | Croxall, Fred. |
| Barr, John | Bromer, Stephen | Campbell, John |
| Brown, John | Bowman, John | Coone, Philip |
| Bounds, Thos. | Bayrley, Ludwick | Camp, John |

---

* Frederick County was established in 1748, from Calvert and Prince George's counties. At the Constitutional Convention of 1776 it was decided to divide this widely extended and now more or less populous Frederick County into three counties, Washington, Montgomery and Frederick ——." The Oaths of Fidelity and Support for Washington and Montgomery Counties were published in the April *Quarterly* (see pp. 1, 21, Vol. VI), and these 337 signers within the Frederick County lines of 1778 complete these existing records within the bounds of Old Frederick County, 3,573 patriotic citizens.  G.M.B.

Clyne, Danl.
Cryder, John
Clabaugh, John, Jr.
Clabaugh, Chas.
Cover, Yost
Cross, George
Clapsaddle, Michl.
Clapsaddle, John
Clapsaddle, George
Capell, Peter
Carmichl. John
Caster, Jacob

Dover, Geo.
Dooinbaugh, Jno.
Dodson, Thos.
Demorey, Jno.
Drumbo, Conrad
Dawson, Benja.
Diffendaller, Mike
Dustman, Martin
Deboy, Joseph

Edwards, Robert
Eck, Maths.
Edwards, John
Elder, Guy
Englar, Jacob

Fligh, Nal
Frazer, Jonthn.
Frye, Isaac
Farmwald, L.
Frye, Abrm.
Frazer, Thos.
Faris, John
Flegle, Chas.
Ferver, Philip
Finnesee, William
Friddle, Jno.
Fervor, Leonard
Foeach, Danl.
Forman, John
Forman, Jacob
Foglesong, George
Faughman, John

Grammer, Jacob
Griffith, Chisholm
Gotard, Valentine
Garrett, Barton
Goiste, Allen
Garrett, John
Gover, Danl.
Green, Henry

Heffner, Jas.
Huffan, David
Hill, Joseph, Jr.
Huff, Philip
Hilton, John
Hilton, James
Hilton, James, Sr.
Huff, Jacob
Hardy, Wm.
Hessong, Balser
Huston, Thos.
Hockman, John
Hart, Christr.
Hull, John
Hinton, Richd.
Hardman, Henry
Hayes, Jonathan
Harnicker, John

Harnicker, Isaac
Houstatter, Francis
Hall, Andw., Jr.
Harlin, James
Hawn, George
Halfpenny, Thos.
Hildebridle, Jacob
Hoyle, Fredk.
Hilton, Freeman
Harrison, John
Hill, Joseph, Sr.
Hill, Thomas
Hamott, Jas.
Hamilton, John
Hawn, George
Hawne, Michael
Hagman, George
Hadon, William
Heckathorn, Jacob
Hagan, Alxnd., Jr.
Hagan, Alexndr., Sr.
   took Oath Before Col. Blany.

Ireland, Alerd
Ihenbury, John
Ironbroad, John Yost

Johnstone, Henry

Kavity, Geo.
Knol, Thos.
Kemp, Jacob
Kendall, Aaron
Keisey, Henry
Kemp, Leonard

Ledsharn, Paul
Leather, John
Lemmon, John
Longsworth, Solomon
Lawfer, Gudlip
Long, Jacob
Link, Nicholas
Loyd, Thomas
Logsdon, John, Jr.
Logsdon, Edw.
Lambert, Balson
Loye, Fred.

Mantz, Peter
Mount, Thos.
Mills, Chas.
Miller, Conrad
Marshall, Geo.
Miller, Danl.
Mifford, Jas.
Mikesell, Andrew
Mathew, Conrad
Miller, Wm.
Myers, Henry
Melton, James
Magruder, Jno.
McLane, Jno.
Moore, Jno.
McNeill, Jno.
McKelom, Wm.
McClain, Josua
Mounikey, Joseph
McCartey, Wm.
Miller, Michael
Miller, Adam
Myer, David
McKean, Joseph
Mathews, Jacob

McLain, Joseph
Maddon, Fred
Miller, Anthony
McMullen, Patrick
Mathews, Philip
Mathews, John
Magruder, James, Jr.
Miller, Luds.
Myer, Sebastian

Nicholls, John
Neede, George
Newcomer, John
Night, Wm.
Nighoff, Fred.

Oll, Adam
Owler, Andrew
Orndorff, Conrad
Ohavin, Christ
Ohavin, Conrad
Ogle, Thos.
Owle (Als, Aler) Danl.
Owler, Phillip

Paterson, Joseph
Pickenbaugh, Geo., Lo.
Polhower, Sand
Panter, John
Panter, Peter
Panter, Jacob
Post, Val.
Payne, Frail
Painter, George
Pain, George
Philpott, Barton

Queen, William

Ramsey, Wm.
Roadabush, Danl.
Ricker, Peter
Riner, Geo.
Runkle, Jacob
Reintzell, Anthy
Roberts, John
Roades, Jacob
Reese, Andr.
Reese, Fred.
Reese, ————

Smith, Godfrey
Shaver, Adam
Smith, Philip
Scott, Geo.
Studey, Peter
Sergeant, James, Sr.
Shirts, George
Sleagle, Henry
Snuke, Jno.
Sage, Thos.
Snyder, Mike
Staley, Henry
Stilbey, Peter
Scott, Samuel
Sergeant, Elisha
Seihfeet, Geo.
Sigirt, Geo.
Smith, John
Sigerfoose, Geo.
Simson, Richd.
Steel, Geo.
Sellman, Babar
Sinn, Jacob
Shilling, Conrad

Shaffer, Conrad
Shaleer, Peter
Super, Christr.
Snowfer, John
Schnertzell, George

Thomas, Gabriel
Tippery, Jacob
Turner, Charles
Thresher, Jno.
Trout, Mike
Thomas, John

(U V None.)

Weaver, Conrad
Wolverton, Charles
Wayner, Bernard N.

Waskey, Augustus
Wagoner, Mike, Jr.
Williams, Thos.
Williams, Wm.
Warner, Peter, Jr.
Warner, Peter, Sr.
Warble, Philis
Weller, John, Jr.
Woolverton, Isaac
Weller, John
Weller, Phillis
Weller, Henry
Woolf, Peter
Willson, Mathew
Wock, John
Woolf, Isaac
Wertenbaker, Adam

Woolfe, George
Weaver, Jas.
Wootsell, Jacob

Yesterday, Christn.
Yesterday, Christn., Jr.
Yost, Jno. H. D.
Young, James
Yesterday, Martin
Young, John
Young, Casper
Young, John, Jr.
Yates, Thomas
Yeast, Phillis
Young, Peter

Zacharias, Danl.

### A List of those who took the affirmation as directed aforesaid.

Barger, Peter
Wygnan, Phillis C., and took
  Oath since, Casper Copd. J.
John Young.
Chamberlain, John
Chamberlain, Jeremiah

Dofler, Peter
Eab, Christn.
Hull, Ano. W.
Hoffman, Peter
Houck, John
Jamison, Samuel

Patterson, Robert
Peer, Philip
Reader, Mike
Steiner, Jacob
Shutter, Christn.
Shaler, George

### Took the Oath by the Court.

Komig, Peter, Jr.
Komig, Gilbert

Komig, Lewis

Komig, Fred.

---

## OATH OF FIDELITY AND SUPPORT TAKEN BEFORE JUSTICE JOHN LAWRENCE, 5 MARCH, 1778—98 CITIZENS.*

"I do swear" etc., the full oath is published on pp. 1, 11., so help me God."

| | | | | | | |
|---|---|---|---|---|---|---|
| 1 | Wood, Basil | 34 | Mobberly, John | 66 | Lee, Richard |
| 2 | Ensey, James | 35 | Davis, Willm. son of Waltr. | 67 | Condon, William |
| 3 | Coombs, Jno. Bapt. | 36 | Winenton, Robert | 68 | Chapman, Nathan |
| 4 | Wood, Charles | 37 | Becraft, Peter Senr. | 69 | Shivers, John Junr. |
| 5 | Braselton, Isaac | 38 | Mason, Jonathan, | 70 | Burkit, William |
| 6 | Murphin, John | 39 | Hall, Nicholas | 71 | Springer, Jacob |
| 7 | Baker, Henry | 40 | Wolf, John | 72 | Cheyney, Charles |
| 8 | Gobbel, George | 41 | Burckhart, Chrisr. | 73 | McDaniel, John |
| 9 | Becraft, John | 42 | Ingman, Edmund | 74 | Ensey, Richard |
| 10 | Shriner, John | 43 | Wolfe, Henry | 75 | Becraft, Benj. |
| 11 | Moore, Abram Ju. | 44 | Clay, George | 76 | Hall, Joseph |
| 12 | Nail, John | 45 | Bradshear, William Jun. | 77 | Hall, Elijah |
| 13 | Fernhaver, John Chris. | 46 | Anderson, Willm. (son | 78 | Baker, Rezin |
| 14 | Smedley, Geo Fredk. | | Absalom) | 79 | Murray, Edwd. |
| 15 | Cyger, George | 47 | Young, James | 80 | Swinchet, Job |
| 16 | Lindsey, Anthony | 48 | Hamilton, James | 81 | Talbott, Richd. |
| 17 | Eberly, Andrew | 49 | Hamilton, John | 82 | Barnes, Leavin |
| 18 | Monohon, Thomas | 50 | Barnes, John | 83 | Barnes, Philemon |
| 19 | Condon, David | 51 | Stevens, Charles C. | 84 | Harrison, Willm. |
| 20 | Adams, George | 52 | Horner, Richard | 85 | McDaniel, Redmund |
| 21 | Stripe, Jacob | 53 | Kindall, William | 86 | Shivers, Thomas |
| 22 | Koontz, Jacob | 54 | Hyatt, Meshaih | 87 | Harrison, Willm. Jun. |
| 23 | Peterson, Henry | 55 | Covell, Jerimiah | 88 | McLain, Willm. |
| 24 | Metcalf, Thomas | 56 | Smith, George | 89 | Awmon, Michael |
| 25 | Becraft, Abram | 57 | Moberly, Lewis | 90 | Hearin, John |
| 26 | Becraft, Peter, Jun. | 58 | Crouch, James | 91 | Beale, Benjn. |
| 27 | Becraft, George, Jun. | 59 | Miller, Nicholas | 92 | Hazlet, Willm. |
| 28 | Tyser, James | 60 | Wright, Philip | 93 | Fellows, Richd. |
| 29 | McDaniel, Joseph | 61 | Davis, Philip | 94 | Wheeler, Thos. |
| 30 | Begold, Willm. | 62 | Humphrey, Owen | 95 | Poole, Henry |
| 31 | Israel, John | 63 | Cooke, William | 96 | Cannon, James |
| 32 | Grimes, Joshua | 64 | Ensey, John | 97 | McDaniel, Francis |
| 33 | Gandy, Jacob | 65 | Davey, Alex. W. | 98 | Duleney, Peter |

I hereby Certify that this is a true Copy taken from the Text Book kept by me, and that the above and aforegoing persons have taken and subscribed the Oath of Fidelity, Agreeable to the directions of an Act of Assembly for the better security of the Government, given under my Hand this 5 Mar. 1778. (Signed)

JNO. LAWRENCE.

* Carefully compared with the original, preserved by the Maryland Historical Society, by Mr. Robert F. Hayes, Jr., Acting Librarian, and by Mr. Charles Fickus. Surname is first given to facilitate reference, and to conform to the preceding Oaths.

*UNPUBLISHED REVOLUTIONARY RECORDS OF PRINCE GEORGE'S COUNTY, LOYAL CIVIL SERVICES FROM APRIL 19, 1775, TO SEPT. 8, 1783.*

### By Caleb Clarke Magruder, Jr., Upper Marlboro, Md.*

"At a County Court of the Right Honorable Henry Harford Esqr,ᵃ Absolute Lord and proprietary of the province of Maryland, etc., Held at Upper Marlborough Town in and for said County on the fourth Tuesday and Twenty-third day of August in the third year of his Lordships Dominion and in the year Seventeen hundred and Seventy-four.

"Present the Worshipful Joshua Beall, William Lock Weems, John Read Magruder, Richard Henderson, Alexander Symmer, Jeremiah Magruder, Thomas Gantt, Jr., James Crow, Christopher Lowndes, John Baynes, Alexander Howard Magruder, Thomas Clagett, Luke Marbury, David Craufurd, Gentlemen Justices by his Lordships Commission in and for the County aforesaid Lawfully authorized and Assigned."

Ralph Forster, Sheriff; Thomas Sim Lee, Clerk of the County. (Liber DD. 1, at 447.) Nathaniel Suit, Constable. (Ibid at 450.)

Although services of the above antedate the Battle of Lexington, April 19, 1775, they were appointed for the ensuing year from August, 1774; and probably so served since their names, with the exception of Luke Marbury, appear as Justices of the Quorum at the next ensuing county court, as does that of the county clerk.

"At a County Court———Held at Upper Marlborough Town——— on the fourth Tuesday and twenty-eighth day of March —in the year Seventeen Hundred and seventy-five.

"Present the Worshipful Joshua Beall, Christopher Lowndes, William Lock Weems, David Craufurd, Alexander Symmer, John Harrison, James Crow, John Baynes, John Read Magruder, Richard Henderson, Thomas Gantt, Jr., Thomas Clagett, Trueman Skinner, Jeremiah Magruder, Alexander Howard Magruder, Gentlemen Justices......" Frank Leeke, Sheriff; Thomas Sim Lee, Clerk of the County. (Liber BB1 at 364.)

"Ralph Forster Sheriff as aforesaid Returns to the Court here the Ensuing Pannel of the Grand Jurors being by him this day Returnable to Wit: Charles Burgess [Foreman], Francis Wheat, Jonathan Burch Junr, John McDaniel, James Alder, John Ramsay Hodges, William Bowie the third, Baruch Duckett, Fielder Bowie, Edward Boteler, James Wilson, Edward Swann, William Watson, Thomas Crawford, Henry Duley, John Fergusson, Nathan Orme ......" All indictments returned by Grand Jury were signed by Thomas Jenings, Attorney-General. (Ibid.)

At a County Court held in and for Prince George's County, in the Town of Upper Marlborough on the third Tuesday and twentieth day of May in the year Seventeen hundred and Seventy-seven by and before The Worshipful Joshua Beall, David Craufurd, Thomas Clagett, Alexander Howard Magruder, Richard Henderson, Fielder Bowie, George Lee, Thomas Williams, Thomas Boyd, William Lyles, Gentlemen, Justices duly Commissioned, Assigned and Qualified.

---

* For more than thirty-five years many of the records containing the Court Proceedings of Prince George's County, Maryland, have been practically lost under a mass of debris in the attic of the county court house. Recently Mr. S. D. Hall, Clerk, authorized Mr. Leroy S. Boyd and Mr. C. C. Magruder, Jr., to institute a search which resulted in the recovery of most of the records, including all but one subsequent to March term, 1775, and prior to May term, 1777, of the Revolutionary period, (1696-1783, organization of the county, etc., lacking one Revolutionary volume, and these volumes are available in the Clerk's office.)

a Henry Harford was the natural son of Frederick, last Lord Baltimore, and as such was "proprietary" of Maryland, but he did not bear the title of Lord Baltimore.

Thomas Duckett, Sheriff. (Liber EE2 at 1.)

"Colonel Joshua Beall Esqr. produces to the Court here the following Commission of the peace which Was Read in open Court to wit: The State of Maryland to Joshua Beall, William Lock Weems, David Craufurd, John Read Magruder, William Beanes, Jeremiah Magruder, Thomas Clagett, Luke Marbury, Trueman Skinner, Alexander Howard Magruder, Richard Henderson, Thomas Gantt Junr, Thomas Trueman, Richard Duckett, Osburn Sprigg, Robert Darnall, Fielder Bowie, George Lee, Jonathan Slator, Humphrey Belt, Benjamin Hall, (son of Francis), Thomas Williams. Thomas Macgill, Thomas Boyd, William Lyles, William Berry, Notley Young, James Mullikin, James Beck and Thomas Richardson of Prince George's County Greeting Be it known that Reposing great Trust and Confidence in your knowledge Integrity and Love of Justice You and every of you jointly and severally are appointed and assigned Justices of Prince George's County Court to do equal Right and Justice according to the Laws of this State in every Case in which you shall act as Justice freely without Sale fully without any Denial and speedily without Delay and you and every three or more of you are assigned the Justices of Prince George's County Court to Execute the same office Justly Honestly and Faithfully according to Law until you shall be duly discharged from your said office. Given under the Seal of the State of Maryland this twenty-first day of April Seventeen hundred and Seventy-seven. Witness the Honorable Richard Sprigg Esqr. Chancellor (Ibid.) Richard Sprigg Chancellor."

Richard Henderson and Thomas Williams qualified as Justices before "Col. Joshua Beall" May 7 and May 9, 1777, respectively. (Ibid) Before Richard Henderson there qualified, Joshua Beall, May 7; William Berry, May 19; David Craufurd, Alexander Howard Magruder, Thomas Boyd, George Lee, Thomas Williams and Fielder Bowie, May 20, 1777. (Ibid at 2.)

Thomas Clagett qualified before William Lyles Junr May 20, 1777. (Ibid.)

William Lyles [Jr.] qualified before Thomas Clagett May 20, 1777. (Ibid.)

"The Justices Aforesaid" Appointed John Read Magruder Clerk of the County who qualified as such May term, 1777. (Ibid.)

Thomas Duckett qualified as Sheriff May term, 1777. (Ibid.)

Constables for the several hundreds of the county appointed for "the present year:" Thomas Boteler, Mattapany; Richard Brightwell, Prince Frederick; John McDaniel, King George's; Francis Wheat, Piscattaway; Walter Williams, Junior, Collington; Richard Keen Scott, Grubb; Francis Hamilton, Mount Calvert; Zephaniah Lowe, Western Branch; Haswell Magruder, New Scotland; John Lansdale Junr, Patuxent; William Pearce, Rock Creek; William Wilson Selby, Eastern Branch; Zephaniah Owen, Upper Marlborough and Charlotte; George Bence, Bladensburgh; Caleb Clarke, Horsepen; Henry Webb, Nottingham; Thomas Wilcoxen, Hynson; Samuel Lanham, Oxon.

Overseers of the Highways appointed for "the present year:" Ignatius Price, New Scotland, upper part; Isaac Sansbury, same, second; Thomas Owen Williams, same, third; Matthew Wigfield, same, lower; Austin Allen, Collington, upper; Joseph Brashears, same, second; Joseph Ramsey Hodges, same, third; Benjamin Jacob, same, fourth; Elisha Berry, Mount Calvert, upper; Joseph Selby, same, lower; Charles Eversfield, same, third; Francis Piles, Western Branch; Tilgham Hilleary, same, upper; Mordecai Burgess, same, middle; John Manley same, lower; John Clark Sprigg, lower division, lower; Basil Beall, Patuxent, lower; Mareen Howard Duvall, same, upper; Elisha Queen, same, fourth; John Lansdale, same, middle; Jeremiah Riley, Rock Creek, upper; Richard Queen, same, lower; John Pearie, Eastern Branch, lower; Richard Simmons Junr, Patuxent; Robert Hooker, Mattapany, upper; William Morton, same, middle; Moses Orme, same, lower; Jesse Hellen, same, back; Joseph Litchworth, Prince Frederick; Patrick Beall, Piscattaway, upper; William Wilcoxen, same, middle; Gales Dyer, same fifth; Robert Darnall, same, lower; Richard

Stonestreet, Riverside; John Talbott, Jericho precincts; John Bowling, King George's, lower; Edward Edelen, same, middle; James Bonifant, same, third; John Wynn, same, back; William Foard, Junr., same, last; John Webster, same. lower division, lower; David Ross, Bladensburgh.
(Ibid at 3 and 4.)

At a County Court held at Upper Marlborough Town, August 26, 1777, and by adjournment on October 21, 1777.

Present: Joshua Beall, David Craufurd, Richard Henderson, William Berry, Alexander Howard Magruder, Thomas Boyd and James Mullikin, Gentlemen, justices, commissioned, qualified etc. (Liber EE2 at 5.)

Thomas Duckett, Sheriff. John Read Magruder, Clerk of the county. (Ibid.)

"Colonel Joshua Beall" read commissions as Justices of the Peace for the following, Joshua Beall, Christopher Lowndes, William Lock Weems, David Craufurd, William Beanes, Jeremiah Magruder, Thomas Clagett, Luke Maroury, Trueman Skinner, Alexander Howard Magruder, Richard Henderson, Thomas Gantt, Jr., Thomas Trueman, Richard Duckett, Jr., Osburn Sprigg, Robert Darnall, Fielder Bowie, George Lee, Jonathan Slator, Humphrey Belt, Benjamin Hall, son of Francis, Thomas Williams, Thomas MacGill, Thomas Boyd, William Lyles, William Berry, Notley Young, James Mullikin, James Beck and Thomas Richardson. Said commissions were signed by Richard Sprigg, Chancellor of Maryland. (Ibid.)

Grand Jurors: James Hawkins [Foreman], John Smith, Samuel Lusby, John Evans, Richard Neal, Michael Lowe, Thomas Sansbury, Isaac Sansbury, James Moore, Joshua Clarke, Jr., Gilbert Falconer, Clement Hill, Jr., Joseph Clarke, Richard Ball, Philip Turner. (Ibid at 5 and 6.)

William Berry qualified as Justice before Joshua Beall, July 1, 1777. (Ibid at 10.)

John Tilley, Bladensburgh hundred, and Mareen Duvall, Horsepen hundred, appointed Constables of their respective hundreds for present year, 1777. (Ibid at 11.)

John Lansdale, Jr., Joseph White Clagett and John Brashears, son of John, cited to show cause why they did not officiate as Constables. (Ibid.)

George Wells, Jr., appointed Constable, Patuxent hundred, for present year (Ibid.)

Joshua Beall and Christopher Lowndes qualified as Justices, June 16, 1777, and Thomas Williams as Justice, June 28, 1777, before Richard Henderson. (Ibid.)

James Mullikin and Benjamin Hall, son of Francis, qualify as Justices (Ibid at 12.)

At a County Court held at Upper Marlborough Town, November 25, 1777.

Present: Joshua Beall, David Craufurd, Thomas Clagett, Trueman Skinner, Alexander Howard Magruder, Thomas Gantt, Jr., Fielder Bowie, Thomas Williams, Thomas Boyd, William Lyles, Jr., William Berry, James Mullikin, and Thomas Macgill, Gentlemen, Justices, commissioned, qualified etc. (Ibid at 29.)

Thomas Duckett, Sheriff. John Read Magruder, Clerk of the county. (Ibid.)

Grand Jurors: Thomas Dent [Foreman], Richard Dent, Richard Ball, Elisha Lanham, Francis Clement Dyer, Alexander Soper, Basil Wilson, Azariah Gatton, Abraham Boyd, Joseph Clarke, Thomas Blanford, William Ray, Walter Queen, James Moore, James Wilson, Alexander Duvall and Charles Clagett. (Ibid.)

Constables for the several hundreds of the county "appointed for the present year:" Thomas Hoye, Mattapany; Richard Brightwell, Prince Frederick; Thomas Stevens, King George's; Francis Wheat, Piscattaway; Isaac Simmons, Collington; Francis Boone, Grub; John Selby, Mount Calvert; Cornelius Duvall, Western Branch; Haswell Magruder, New Scotland; William Nicholls, Jr., Patuxent; Walter Queen, Rock Creek; Isaac Walker, Jr., Eastern Branch, William Hutchison, Upper Marlborough; John Tilly, Bladensburgh; Caleb Clarke, Horsepen; William Keadle, Charlotte; Henry Webb, Nottingham; Caleb Hurley, Hynson; Samuel Lanham, Oxon. (Ibid at 30.)

Overseers of the Highways appointed for the ensuing year: Ignatius Price, New Scotland, upper part; John Scissell, same second; James Tannihill, same, third; Matthew Wigfield, same, lower; Charles Clagett, Collington, upper; Joseph Brashears, same, second; Joseph Ramsay Hodges, same, third; Richard Higgins, same, fourth; Elisha Berry, Mount Calvert, upper; Joseph Selby, same lower; Thomas Hamilton, same, third; Thomas Clagett, Western Branch; Tilgham Hilleary, same, upper; Mordecai Burgess, same, middle; John Manley, same, lower; John Clark Sprigg, same, lower division, lower; William Nicholls, of Clarke, Patuxent, upper; Elisha Green, same, fourth; Thomas Plummer, same, middle; Thomas Brashears, same, lower; Jeremiah Riley, Rock Creek, upper; Richard Queen, same lower; John Perrie, Eastern Branch, lower; Richard Lansdale, Patuxent; Robert Hooker, Mattapany, upper; William Morton, same, middle; Thomas Smith, same, lower; James Haddock Waring, same, back; Levin Covington, Prince Frederick; Patrick Beall, Piscattaway, upper; William Wilcoxen, same, middle; John Davidson, same, fifth; Samuel Lusby, same, lower; Richard Stonestreet, same, riverside; Richard Ball, Jericho precincts; John Bowling, King George's, lower; Edward Edelen, same, middle; Nathaniel Newton, same, third; John Wynn, same back; William Foard, Jr., same last; John Webster, same, lower division, lower; Adam Craig, Bladensburgh. (Ibid at 30 and 31.)

George Lee qualified as Justice before Thomas Clagett, August 8, 1777. (Ibid at 31.)

Thomas Sim Lee allowed fees as late Clerk of the County. (Ibid at 32.)

Clement Wheeler, Commissioner of the Alms House. (Ibid.)

Thomas Duckett allowed fees as Sheriff of the county. (Ibid.)

Ralph Forster allowed fees as late Sheriff of the county. (Ibid.)

John Read Magruder allowed fees as Clerk of the county. (Ibid at 33.)

Henry Nicholls, Cryer of the Court. (Ibid.)

Benjamin Wailes, Inspector of tobacco at Magruder's warehouse. (Ibid.)

Daniel Clarke and Joshua Clarke, Inspectors of tobacco at Queen Anne warehouse. (Ibid.)

Trueman Skinner and Thomas Macgill qualify as Justices, November, 1777. (Ibid at 37.)

Robert Pack Brookes appointed Drummer for the ensuing year, November, 1777. (Ibid at 39.)

At a County Court held at Upper Marlborough Town March 24, 1778. Present: David Craufurd, Thomas Williams, James Beck, Fielder Bowie, Osburn Sprigg, James Mullikin, Thomas Boyd, George Lee, Thomas Macgill, Alexander Howard Magruder, Trueman Skinner, Thomas Clagett, William Lyles, Thomas Gantt, Jr., Gentlemen, Justices, commissioned, qualified, etc. (Ibid at 52.) Thomas Duckett, Sheriff. John Read Magruder, Clerk of the county. (Ibid.)

Grand Jurors: Thomas Dent [Foreman], Charles Burgess, Basil Beall, George Fraser Magruder, Johnson Michael Riley, Jeremiah Brashears, Henry Hardey, Jr., Henry Spalding, James Bonifant, John Lowe, Jr., Josias Beall, Richard Kirby, Jesse Hellen, Thomas Boteler, Isaac Sansbury and Basil Crawford (Ibid.)

James Beck and Thomas Boyd qualified as Justices before Thomas Williams, June 14, 1777. (Ibid at 54.)

Osburn Sprigg qualified as Justice before David Craufurd January 25, 1778, (Ibid.)

Samuel Tyler qualified as Register of Wills before David Craufurd February 21, 1778, (Ibid.)

John Read Magruder qualified as Clerk of the county, Feb. 28, 1778. (Ibid at 55.)

Thomas Duckett qualified as Sheriff before David Craufurd February 28, 1778, (Ibid.)

James Harvey appointed Constable, Mount Calvert hundred, for ensuing year. (Ibid at 57.)

At a County Court held at Upper Marlborough Town August 25, 1778. Present: Joshua Beall, Christopher Lowndes, David Craufurd. Thomas Clagett, Trueman Skinner, Alexander Howard Magruder, Richard Henderson, Thomas Gantt, Jr., Fielder Bowie, Thomas Williams, Thomas Boyd, William Berry, James Mullikin, James Beck, Gentlemen, Justices, commissioned, qualified etc. (Liber EE2 at 90.)

Thomas Duckett, Sheriff. John Read Magruder, Clerk of the county. (Ibid.)

Grand Jurors: Thomas Dent [Foreman], Johnson Michael Riley, Levi Gantt, John Lowe, Jr., Thomas Crawford, Richard Kirby, Nathan Prather, Thomas Sansbury, Richard Dent, Joseph Smith, Isaac Smith, William Bowie the third, Joseph Wilson, Sr., Levin Wilcoxen, Soloman Groves, James Wilson, William Ray, Philip Turner and John Talbott. (Ibid.)

Grand Jury found that "Daniel Stephenson hath left this State since the fourteenth day of August Seventeen hundred and seventy-five to avoid taking an active part in defense of this State." (Ibid at 93.)

Same findings returned against Robert Findlay, John Campbell, Rev. Jonathan Boucher and Rev. Henry Addison. It was ordered that transcripts of same be forwarded to the Council of Safety. (Ibid at 94.)

Rinaldo Johnson appointed Prosecutor for the county. (Ibid.)

Hugh Lyon qualified as Deputy Clerk of the county before David Craufurd, July 29, 1778. (Ibid at 95.)

Barton Lucas, Coroner, June 16, 1778. (Ibid at 97.)

Eliza Knight presented to the Court "that her husband has gone to camp," and she is without subsistence; whereupon the Court allowed her 10 pounds current money. (Ibid.)

At a County Court held at Upper Marlborough Town November 24, 1778, January 19, 1779, and by adjournment February 22, 1779. Present: Joshua Beall, David Craufurd, John Harrison, Thomas Clagett, Trueman Skinner, Alexander Howard Magruder, Fielder Bowie, Thomas Williams, Thomas Macgill, Thomas Boyd, William Berry, James Beck, Henry Rozer. Frank Leek, Samuel Chew Hepburn, John Smith Brookes, Gentlemen, Justices, commissioned, qualified etc. (Ibid at 269.)

Thomas Duckett, Sheriff. John Read Magruder, Clerk of the county. (Ibid.)

Grand Jurors: Thomas Dent [Foreman], Joshua Clarke, Joshua Clarke, Jr., Charles Burgess, William Taylor, William Harvey, Henry Brookes, John Eversfield, William Ray, John Lowe, Jr., Samuel Lusbey, Jonathan Burch, Jr., James Edmonston, Josias Beall, William Hall, Alexander Crawford, Richard Kirby, Richard Ball and James Moore. (Ibid.)

"Colonel Joshua Beall" produced and read in open Court commissions as Justices of the Peace for the following (November Court):

Joshua Beall, Christopher Lowndes, William Lock Weems, David Craufurd, John Hanson, Richard Henderson, Thomas Gantt, Jr., Luke Marbury. Thomas Clagett, Trueman Skinner, Alexander Howard Magruder. Osburn Sprigg, Fielder Bowie, George Lee, Benjamin Hall, son of Francis, Thomas Williams, Thomas Macgill, Thomas Boyde, William Lyles, William Berry, James Mullikin, James Beck, Henry Rozer, Frank Leeke, Samuel Hepburn, John Brown,

Abraham Boyd and John Smith Brookes. Commissions signed by John Rogers, Chancellor of Maryland. (Ibid at 271.)

The following qualified as Justices: Joshua Beall, Thomas Williams, Thomas Macgill, James Beck, Samuel Chew Hepburn, John Smith Brookes, Fielder Bowie, Frank Leeke, Thomas Boyd, David Craufurd, Henry Rozer, Alexander Howard Magruder, John Harrison, Thomas Clagett, William Berry. (Ibid at 272.)

Thomas Gantt, Jr., qualified as Justice before Alexander Howard Magruder, February 28, 1779. (Ibid at 278.)

Rinaldo Johnson produced his power of attorney as Prosecutor for the county from Luther Martin, Attorney-General of Maryland, dated January 16, 1779. (Ibid.)

At a County Court held at Upper Marlborough Town, March 23, 1779. Present: Joshua Beall, David Craufurd, Richard Henderson, Fielder Bowie, Thomas Macgill, William Berry, Frank Leeke, Samuel Chew Hepburn, Abraham Boyd, John Smith Brookes, Gentlemen, Justices, commissioned, qualified etc. (Ibid at 356.)

Thos. Duckett, Sheriff. John Read Magruder, Clerk of the county. (Ibid.)

Grand Jurors: Edward Sprigg [Foreman], William Bowie the third, Zachariah Berry, Johnson Michael Riley, Charles Maddocks, Thomas Stevens, Josias Wilcoxen, Joseph Wilson, Sr., Thomas Baden, Henry Hill, Jr., Nicholas Davis, John Everfield, Jr., Andrew Beall, Richard Queen, John Hamilton, Thomas Adams and William Ray. (Ibid.)

Abraham Boyd and John Brown qualified as Justices. (Ibid at 357.)

"Richard Henderson produces to the Court here his account against the County for an allowance for Administering the Oath of Fidelity and is allowed six pounds current money in the present County Levy for that purpose." (Ibid.)

Barton Lucas allowed for services as Coroner (Ibid.)

At a County Court held at Upper Marlborough Town August 24, 1779. Present: Joshua Beall, David Craufurd, John Harrison, Fielder Bowie, Thomas Williams, Thomas Macgill, Thomas Boyd, William Lyles, William Berry, James Mullikin, James Beck, Frank Leeke, Samuel Hepburn, John Brown, John Smith Brookes, Gentlemen, Justices, commissioned, qualified etc. (Ibid at 431.)

Thos. Duckett, Sheriff. John Read Magruder, Clerk of the county. (Ibid.)

Grand Jurors: John Addison [Foreman], John Macgill, Johnson Michael Riley, William Moore, Joseph Wilson, Thomas Harvey, John Stone, John Waring, Jacob Duckett, William Taylor, Nicholas Davis, John Baden, John Baden, Jr., William Sprigg Bowie, Richard Beall, Basil Craufurd and Thomas Beall (Ibid.)

At a County Court held at Upper Marlborough Town November 23, 1779 Present: Joshua Beall, William Lock Weems, David Craufurd, John Harrison, Richard Henderson, Thomas Clagett, Alexander Howard Magruder, Fielder Bowie, Thomas Williams, Thomas Macgill, Thomas Boyd, William Lyles, William Berry, James Mullikin, James Beck, Frank Leeke, Samuel Hepburn, John Brown, Abraham Boyd, John Smith Brookes, Gentlemen, Justices, commissioned, qualified etc. (Ibid at 521.)

Thomas Duckett, Sheriff. John Read Magruder, Clerk of the county. (Ibid.)

Grand Jurors: Thomas Dent [Foreman], Richard Ball, Edward Simms, John Waring, William Taylor, Edward Lanham, Basil Waring, Jr., Daniel McLish, Thomas Baden, Joseph Clarke, Edward Villers Harbin, Samuel Jones, Basil Crawford, Peter Carns, William Hall, Charles Burgess, Levin Wilcoxen, James Edmonston. (Ibid.)

Josiah Hatton presented by Grand Jury for "harbouring and secreting William Whitmore a Deserter from the Southern Army." (Ibid.)

Zachariah Owens, sub-sheriff of the county (Ibid at 522.)

Francis Wheat, Thomas Belt, Thomas Hoye, Jr., James Wilson and Richard Brightwell, Constables. (Ibid.)

"Colonel Joshua Beall" produced and read in open Court commissions as Justices of the Peace for the following: Joshua Beall, Christopher Lowndes, William Lock Weems, David Craufurd, John Harrison, Richard Henderson, Thomas Gantt, Jr., Luke Marbury, Thomas Clagett, Trueman Skinner, Alexander Howard Magruder, Osburn Sprigg, Fielder Bowie, George Lee, Thomas Macgill, Thomas Boyd, William Lyles, William Berry, James Mullikin, James Beck, Henry Rozer, Frank Leeke, Samuel Hepburn, John Brown, Abraham Boyd, John Smith Brookes. Commissions signed by John Rogers, Chancellor of Maryland. (Ibid at 524.)

Constables appointed for ensuing year: Thomas Dorsett, son of Thomas, Mattapany hundred; Richard Brightwell, Prince Frederick; Thomas Blacklock, Jr., King George's; Francis Wheat, Piscataway; Walter Hilleary, Collington; Francis Boon, son of Henry, Grubb; John Smith Selby, Mount Calvert; William Moodie, Western Branch; Josiah Beall, New Sctoland; Isaac Lansdale, Patuxent; Aquilla Wheeler, Rock Creek; Ralph Jones, Eastern Branch; Wiseman· Clagett, Upper Marlborough; Peter Carns, Bladensburgh; Frederick Clarke, Horsepen; Wiseman Clagett, Charlotte; George Gantt, Washington; John Evans, Hynson. James Tannihill, Jr., Oxon. (Ibid.)

Overseers of the Highways for ensuing year: Nacey Brashears, New Scotland, upper part; Haswell Magruder, same, second; Nathaniel Pope, Oxon, upper; George Bean, same, lower; Charles Clagett, Collington, upper; Richard Lamar, same, second; Joseph Ramsay Hodges, same, third; Benjamin Duvall the third, same, fourth; Elisha Berry, Mount Calvert, upper; William Newman Dorsett, same, lower; Nicholas Brooke, same, third; Thomas Clagett, Jr., Western Branch; Tilghman Hilleary, same, upper; John Burgess, same, middle; John Manley, same, lower; John Osborn, same, lower division, lower; Benjamin Gaither, Patuxent, upper; Elisha Green, same, fourth; Francis Bird, same, middle; Basil Beall, same, lower; William Fergusson, Rock Creek, upper; Thomas Pierce, same, lower; Thomas Scissell, Eastern Branch, lower; Archibald Ellson, Patuxent; Jonas Austin, Mattapany, upper; Benjamin Baden, same, middle; Thomas Smith, same, lower; Samuel Poston, same, back; Levin Covington, Prince Frederick; John Lowe, Jr., Piscattaway, upper; William Wilcoxen, same, middle; Soloman Lanham, same, fifth; Thomas Edelen, same, lower; George Hatton, same, riverside; Richard Ball, Jericho precincts; John Bowling, King George's, lower; Edward Edelen, same, middle; Nathaniel Newton, same, third; John Wynn, same, back; William Foard, same, last; John Webster, same. lower division, lower; Adam Craig, Bladensburgh. (Ibid.)

Thomas Williams presented his bond as Sheriff which was approved by the Court. (Ibid.)

Rinaldo Johnson allowed fees as Prosecutor of the county. (Ibid at 528.)

Same as to Samuel Tyler, Register of Wills. (Ibid.)

Same as to John Read Magruder, Clerk of the county. (Ibid.)

Same as to Hugh Lyon; Deputy Clerk of the county. (Ibid.)

Same as to Thomas Duckett, Sheriff of the county. (Ibid.)

Same as to Henry Nicholls, Cryer of the Court. (Ibid.)

At a County Court held at Upper Marlborough Town March 28, 1780.

Present: Joshua Beall, Frank Leeke, Samuel Hepburn, Henry Rozer, David Craufurd, James Beck, Alexander Howard Magruder, William Lyles, James Mullikin, Abraham Boyd, Thomas Clagett, Thomas Boyd, William Berry, John Brown, John Smith Brookes, Gentlemen, Justices, commissioned, qualified etc. (Liber EE2 at 556.)

Thomas Williams, Sheriff. John Read Magruder, Clerk of the county. (Ibid.)

Grand Jurors: Joshua Clarke [Foreman], Thomas Owen Williams, Sam-

uel Lusby, Cornelius Hurley, Thomas Sansbury, John Baden, Henry Hilleary, Joseph Clarke, Zachariah Berry, Thomas Ramsay Hodges, Edward Magruder, Joseph Willson, Sr., Charles Maddocks, John Wheat, John Waring, William Bowie the third, Josias Sprigg Wilson, George Moore, James Drane. (Ibid.)
    William Lyles referred to as Major, 1780. (Ibid at 558.)
    Rinaldo Johnson, Prosecutor for the county. (Ibid at 569.)
    At a County Court held at Upper Marlborough Town August 22, 1780.
    Present; Joshua Beall, William Lock Weems, David Craufurd, Thomas Clagett, Alexander Howard Magruder, Fielder Bowie, Thomas Macgill, James Mullikin, James Beck, Frank Leeke, Samuel Hepburn, John Brown, Abraham Boyd, John Smith Brookes, Gentlemen, Justices, commissioned, qualified, etc. (Ibid at 629.)
    Thomas Williams, Sheriff. John Read Magruder, Clerk of the county. (Ibid.)
    Grand Jurors: Thomas Dent [Foreman], Johnson Michael Riley, James Waring, Thomas Lyles, Alexander Jefferies, John Baden, Joseph Clarke. Anthony Hardey, Alexander Crawford, Jacob Aldridge, Benjamin Berry, Robert Tyler, Benjamin Prather, Josias S. Wilson, Jesse Duvall, Joshua Clarke, Jr., John Williams. (Ibid.)
    Henry Nicholls appointed Drummer.( Ibid at 637.)
    Benjamin Brookes, late Standard Keeper, ordered to deliver the standard to Robert Baden who qualified as Standard Keeper. (Ibid.)
    Richard Beall referred to as Captain. (Ibid at 639.)
    John Allen Thomas, Prosecutor for the county. (Ibid at 641.)
    At a County Court held at Upper Marlborough Town March 20, 1781.
    Present: Joshua Beall, David Craufurd, John Harrison, Fielder Bowie, Thomas Boyd, James Mullikin, Frank Leeke, Samuel Hepburn, John Brown, John Smith Brookes, Gentlemen, Justices, commissioned, qualified, etc. (Ibid at 665.)
    Thomas Williams, Sheriff. John Read Magruder, Clerk of the county. (Ibid.)
    John Allen Thomas allowed fees as Prosecutor for the county. (Ibid.)
    Same as to Thomas Williams, Sheriff of the county. (Ibid.)
    Same as to John Read Magruder, Clerk of the county. (Ibid.)
    Same as to Henry Nicholls, Cryer of the Court. (Ibid.)
    Same as to Samuel Tyler, Register of Wills. (Ibid.)
    Same as to Robert Baden, Standard Keeper. (Ibid.)
    Thomas Williams qualified as Sheriff. (Ibid at 666.)
    At a County Court held at Upper Marlborough Town March 27, 1781.
    Present. Joshua Beall, David Craufurd, John Harrison, Richard Henderson, Alexander Howard Magruder, Fielder Bowie, Thomas Macgill, Thomas Boyd, James Mullikin, Henry Rozer, Frank Leeke, Samuel Hepburn, John Brown, Abraham Boyd, John Smith Brookes, Gentlemen, Justices, commissioned qualified etc. (Ibid at 667.)
    Thomas Williams, Sheriff. John Read Magruder, Clerk of the county. (Ibid.)
    Grand Jurors: Henry Brookes [Foreman], Tilghman Hilleary, Johnson Michael Riley, James Drane, Thomas R. Hodges, Robert Whitaker, Thomas Stevens, Anthony Hardey, Charles Maddocks, Edward Lanham, Thomas Tilly, Isaac Sansbury, Jonathan Simmons, Thomas Mudd, Ignatius Fenwick, John Waring, Edward Swann, Thomas Adams, Charles R. Hodges. (Ibid.)
    "Col. Joshua Beall" produced and read in open Court Commissions as Justices of the Peace for the following: Joshua Beall, Christopher Lowndes, William Lock Weems, David Craufurd, John Harrison, Richard Henderson, Thomas Gatt [Gantt], Jr., Luke Marbury, Thomas Clagett, Alexander Howard Magruder, Osborn Sprigg, Fielder Bowie, George Lee, Thomas Macgill, Thomas

Boy.l, William Lyles, William Berry, James Mullikin, James Beck, Henry Rozer, Frank Leeke, Samuel Hepburn, John Brown, Abraham Boyd, John Smith Brookes. Commissions signed by John Rogers, Chancellor of Maryland. (Ibid at 668.)

Constables appointed for the ensuing year: Lingan Boteler, Mattapany hundred; Richard Brightwell, Prince Frederick; John Nevitt, Jr., King George's; Francis Wheat, Piscattaway; Walter Hilleary, Collington; Nathaniel O'Neal, Grubb; Thomas Boteler, of Charles, Mount Calvert; William Moodie, Western Branch; James Waring, New Scotland; Isaac Lansdale, Patuxtent; Richard Jameson, Rock Creek; Ralph Jones, Eastern Branch; William Hutchinson, Upper Marlborough; Charles Man (Maw?), Bladensburgh; Samuel Nicholls, Horsepen; Nicholas Blacklock, Charlotte; George Gantt, Washington; George Upton, Hynson; James Tannihill, Jr., Oxon. (Ibid at 669.)

Overseers of the Highways for ensuing year: James Edmonston, New Scotland, upper part; John Robinson, same, second; Nathaniel Pope, Oxon, upper; George Bean, same, lower; William Bowie the third, Collington, upper; Richard Lamar, same, second; Joseph Ramsay Hodges, same, third; Joseph Cross, of George, same, fourth; John Read Magruder, Mount Calvert, upper; William Newman Dorsett, same, lower; Alexis Boone, same, third; Robert Baden, Western Branch; Tilghman Hilleary, same, upper; John Burgess, same middle; John Manley, same, lower; John McKay, same, lower division, lower; Christopher Hyatt, Patuxent, upper; Elisha Green, same, fourth; Francis Bird, same, middle; George Wells, of George, same, lower; William Fergusson, Rock Creek, upper; Thomas Price, same, lower; Thomas Scissell, Eastern Branch, lower; Archibald Elson, Patuxent; Jonas Austin, Mattapany, upper; William Morton, same, middle; Thomas Smith, same, lower; Samuel Poston, same, back; Levin Covington, Prince Frederick; John Lowe, Jr., Piscattaway, upper; Robert Fish, same, middle; William Tennerly, same, fifth; Zachariah Jenkins, same, lower; Charles Jones, same, riverside; Richard Ball, Jericho precincts; John Bowling, King George's, lower; Edward Edelen, same, middle; Nathaniel Newton, same, third; John Wynn, same, back; William Foard, same, last; John Webster, same, lower division, lower; Adam Craig, Bladensburgh. (Ibid.)

At a County Court held at Upper Marlborough Town August 28, 1781: Present: Joshua Beall, David Craufurd, Frank Leeke, John Smith Brookes, Samuel Hepburn, William Berry, Henry Rozer, James Mullikin, Boyd [Thomas or Abraham], John Harrison, Fielder Bowie, Gentlemen, Justices, commissioned, qualified etc., (Ibid at 700.)

Thomas Williams, Sheriff. John Read Magruder, Clerk of the county, (Ibid.)

Grand Jurors: Thomas Owen Williams [Foreman], John Lowe, Jr., Samuel Lusby, Henry Hardey, Edward Villers Harbin, James Ray, Thomas Crawford, Benjamin Berry, Joshua Clarke, Charles Clagett, John Lansdale, Jr., Alexander Jefferies, Robert Baden, Mordecai Burgess, Thomas Baden, Thomas Duvall, Joseph Wilson, Cornelius Hurley, Thomas Ramsay Hodges. (Ibid.)

Thomas Atkin presented by Grand Jury on information of William Mcodie and John Honnis "for harbouring and entertaining Joseph Mockbee a Deserter." (Ibid.)

Judson Coolidge referred to as Captain, August, 1781, (Ibid at 712.)

At a County Court held at Upper Marlborough Town November 27, 1781 Present: Joshua Beall, David Craufurd, Fielder Bowie, Thomas Boyd, William Berry, Frank Leeke, Samuel Hepburn, Abraham Boyd, Gentlemen, Justices, commissioned, qualified, etc. (Ibid at 761.)

Thomas Williams, Sheriff. John Read Magruder, clerk of the county. (Ibid.)

Grand Jurors: Benjamin Brookes [Foreman], John Evans, Joseph Wilson, Thomas Mudd, Joseph White Clagett, Joseph Clarke, Alexander Jefferies,

Walter Evans, Middleton Belt, John McDaniel, Richard Dent, Alexander Soper, Benjamin Belt, Thomas Hewitt, John Eversfield. (Ibid.)

Constables for several hundreds of the county appointed for the ensuing year: Thomas Baden, Mattapany; Richard Brightwell, Prince Frederick; Thomas Blacklock, King George's; Francis Wheat, Piscattaway; James Drane, Jr., Collington; Nathaniel O'Neal, Grubb; Charles Boteler, Mount Calvert; William Moodie, Western Branch; James Waring, New Scotland; Joseph Allen, Patuxent; Abraham Young, Rock Creek; Andrew Beall, Eastern Branch; William Hutchinson, Upper Marlborough; Brian Daily, Bladensburgh; Charles Duvall, Horsepen; Nicholas Blacklock, Charlotte; George Gantt, Washington; Thomas Wilcoxen, Jr., Hynson; George Beall, Jr., Oxon. (Ibid at 762.)

Overseers for the highways: Shadrack Turner, New Scotland, upper part; Thomas Beall, of Ninian, same, second; Richard Marshall, Oxon, upper; George Bean, same, lower; William Bowie the third, Collington, upper; Richard Lamar, same, second; Joseph Ramsay Hodges, same, third; Joseph Cross, of George, same, fourth; Benjamin Brookes, Mount Calvert, upper; William Newman Dorsett, same, lower; Alexis Boone, same, third; Thomas Clagett, Western Branch, Tilghman Hilleary, Western Branch; John Burgess, same, middle; John Manley, same, lower; John McKay, same, lower division, lower; Christopher Hyatt, Patuxent, upper; Elisha Green, same, fourth; Francis Bird, same, middle; Thomas Ramsay Hodges, same, lower; William Fergusson, Rock Creek, upper; David Burns, same, lower; James Beall, Eastern Branch, lower; John Crow, Patuxent; John Ryon, of William, Mattapany, upper; William Morton, same, middle; Thomas Smith, same, lower; Samuel Poston, same, back; Levin Covington, Prince Frederick; John Lowe, Jr., Piscattaway, upper; Ignatius Hardey, same, middle; John Harris Gibbs, same, fifth; Edward Jenkins, same, lower; Charles Jones, riverside; Richard Ball, Jericho precincts; John Bowling, King George's, lower; Edward Edelen, same, middle; Nathaniel Newton, same, third, John Wynn, same, back; William Foard, same, last; John Webster, same, lower division, lower; Christopher Lowndes, Bladensburgh. (Ibid.)

Accounts of Barton Lucas and David Craufurd as Coroners allowed by the Court (Ibid at 765.)

Stead Lowe qualified as under clerk of the county. (Ibid.)

Archibald Boyd acting Prosecutor for the county. (Ibid at 781.)

At a County Court held at Upper Marlborough Town March 26, 1782. Present: Joshua Beall, David Craufurd, Alexander Howard Magruder, Fielder Bowie, Thomas Boyd, William Berry, James Mullikin, Samuel Hepburn, John Brown, Jr., Abraham Boyd, John Smith Brookes, Gentlemen, Justices, commissioned, qualified etc., (Ibid at 783.)

Thomas Williams, Sheriff. John Read Magruder, Clerk of the county. (Ibid.)

Grand Jurors: Thomas Dent [Foreman], Edward Willett, Mordecai Burgess, Joseph Clarke. John Lowe, Jr., John Spalding, Charles Clagett. Charles Ramsay Hodges, Henderson Magruder, Thomas Hewitt, John Turnbull, John Brown, Joseph White Clagett, Benjamin Berry, John Hawkins, Thomas Crawford, Thomas Dyer and Joseph Queen. (Ibid.)

"Col. Joshua Beall" produced and read in open Court commissions as Justices of the peace for the following: Joshua Beall, Christopher Lowndes, William Lock Weems, David Craufurd, John Harrison, Richard Henderson, Thomas Gantt, Jr., Thomas Clagett, Alexander Howard Magruder, Osburn Sprigg, Fielder Bowie, George Lee, Thomas Boyd, William Berry, James Mullikin, James Beck, Henry Rozier, Frank Leeke, Samuel Hepburn, John Brown, Abraham Boyd, John Smith Brookes. Commissions signed by John Rogers. Chancellor of Maryland. (Ibid at 784.)

John Allen Thomas, Prosecutor for the county. (Ibid at 790.)

At a County Court held at Upper Marlborough Town August 27, 1782.

Present: Joshua Beall, David Craufurd, Samuel Hepburn, Frank Leeke, Henry Roser, Thomas Clagett, James Mullikin, Abraham Boyd, Thomas Boyd, James Beck, John Smith Brookes and John Brown, Gentlemen, Justices, commissioned, qualified, etc. Liber (letter obliterated) from Aug. 27, 1782 to Mch. 23, 1784, both dates included, at 1.

Thomas Williams, Sheriff. John Read Magruder, Clerk of the county (Ibid.)

Grand Jurors: Michael Lowe [Foreman], Isaac Sansbury, Richard Isaac, George Moore, Jr., Joseph Clarke, Henry Hill, Jr., Nicholas Brookes, Clement Garner, Joseph Wilson, Jr., John Wheat, Samuel Lusby, Alexander Soper, John R. Hodges, Francis Boone, Cornelius Hurley. (Ibid.)

Edward Jenkins overseer of the highways for lower part of Piscattaway hundred; James Belt same for lower part of Eastern Branch hundred. (Ibid at 2)

Thomas Lyles, Nicholas Blacklock and Henry Humphreys Deputy Sheriffs. (Ibid.)

John Allen Thomas, Prosecutor for the county. (Ibid at 19.)

At a County Court held at Upper Marlborough Town November 26, 1782.

Present: Joshua Beall, David Craufurd, Samuel Hepburn, James Mullikin, John Brown, Thomas Boyd, James Beck, Gentlemen, Justices, commissioned, qualified etc. (Ibid at 77.)

Thomas Williams, Sheriff. John Read Magruder, Clerk of the county. (Ibid.)

Grand Jurors: James Perry [Foreman], (signed Pearre on indictments), Thomas Smith Cox, Walter Trueman Greenfield, Joseph Clarke, Mordecai Burgess, John Smith Selby, Edward Willett, Charles Maddocks, Michael Lowe, John Wheat, Joseph Wilson, Isaac Sansbury, John Jenkins, John R. Hodges, Johnson M. Riley. (Ibid.)

Edward Jenkins overseer of highway, lower part of Piscattaway hundred. (Ibid.)

High Sheriff's bond of John Beall, dated November 25, 1782, filed. He qualified before David Craufurd. (Ibid at 80.)

Theodore Beall qualified as Deputy Sheriff before Joshua Beall; Nicholas Blacklock qualified as Deputy Sheriff before Samuel Hepburn; Zachariah Owen qualified as Deputy Sheriff before James Mullikin. (Ibid.)

Edward Stonestreet qualified as Deputy Collector before Abraham Boyd. (Ibid.)

Michael I. Stone, Prosecutor for the county. (Ibid at 84.)

At a County Court held at Upper Marlborough Town March 25, 1783.

Present: Joshua Beall, David Craufurd, Frank Leeke, Samuel Hepburn, John Smith Brookes, Rinaldo Johnson, James Mullikin, Henry Rozer, John Brown, William Berry, Abraham Boyd, Thomas Boyd, Gentlemen, Justices, commissioned, qualified etc. (Ibid at 109.)

John Beall, Sheriff. John Read Magruder, clerk of the county. (Ibid.)

Grand Jurors: John Waring [Foreman], William Waters, Richard Higgins, Joseph Brashears, Mordecai Burgess, Richard Isaac, Edward Burch, Cornelius Hurley, Clement Gardiner, Henry L. Mudd, Joseph Clarke, Electus Boone, Samuel Lusby, Edward Willett, James Bonifant, Joseph Wilson, William Taylor, John Spalding and Charles Maddox. (Ibid.)

"Col. Joshua Beall" produced and read in open Court commissions as Justices of the Peace for the following; Joshua Beall, Christopher Lowndes, William Lock Weems, David Craufurd, Richard Henderson, Thomas Clagett, Osburn Sprigg, Fielder Bowie, Thomas Boyd, William Berry, James Mullikin, James Beck, Henry Rozer, Frank Leeke, Samuel Hepburn, John Brown, Abraham Boyd, John Smith Brookes and Rinaldo Johnson. Commissions signed by John Rogers, Chancellor of Maryland. (Ibid at 110.)

Alexander Howard Magruder referred to as Captain of the Flying Camp, 1776. (Ibid at 115.)

William Dent Beall qualified before Joshua Beall as Deputy Sheriff. (Ibid at 117.)

Joshua Beall, David Craufurd, Frank Leeke, Samuel Hepburn, John Smith Brookes, Rinaldo Johnson, James Mullikin, Henry Rozer, John Brown, Abraham Boyd, Thomas Boyd, William Berry qualified as Justices. (Ibid at 118.)

Michael I. Stone, Prosecutor for the county. (Ibid at 121.)

At a County Court held at Upper Marlborough Town August 26, 1783. Present: Joshua Beall, David Craufurd, Frank Leeke, Samuel Hepburn, Henry Roser, Abraham Boyd, Thomas Boyd, John Brown, John Smith Brookes, Rinaldo Johnson, Gentlemen, Justices, commissioned, qualified etc. (Ibid at 150.)

John Beall, Sheriff. John Read Magruder, Clerk of the county. (Ibid.)

Grand Jurors: Thomas Dent [Foreman], Moses Orme, Naylor Davis, Benjamin Sedwick Cox, Alexander Jefferies, James Bonifant, William Newman Dorsett, James Perrie, Charles Maddox, James Ramsay Hodges, William White, Zachariah Berry, John Jenkins, Richard Isaac, Edward Willett and Johnson Michael Riley, (Ibid.)

James Swann and Edward Jenkins overseers of highways. (Ibid at 151.)

Joseph Edelen, overseer of highway. (Ibid at 152.)

John Allen Thomas, Prosecutor for the county. (Ibid at 175.)

Joshua Beall referred to as Lieutenant of the Middle Battalion, April 28, and July 17, 1779 (Ibid at 185.)

Leonard Townshend a Constable, April 12, 1783. (Ibid at 193.)

# "BOOK OF PERSONS HAVING TAKEN THE OATH TO SUPPORT GOVERNMENT"

(Oath follows—the same as given upon viii)*

## CALVERT COUNTY, MARYLAND

| | | |
|---|---|---|
| Wilkinson, Joseph | Stallings, Itichd. | Deale, Richard, Jnr. x |
| Grahame, James | Gibson, James | Gibson, Richard x |
| Fitzhugh, Peregne | Austin, Samuel S. | Cox, Jedediah Jnr. |
| King, T[hos.] (Francis?) | Austin, William | ffinton, Richard x |
| Balch, Stephen B. | Boyd, Robert | Smith, John Hamilton |
| Cleland, Thomas | Worthington, Chas., of Nick. | Ward, Itichard |
| Spicknale, John | Donaldson, George | Harrison, Henry |
| Young, Philemon | Brassan, John Jnr. x | Douell, John |
| Cox, Jeremiah x | Lyles, Henry | Cox, John x |
| Richmond, Jno. | Poole, Thomas x | Britain, States x |
| Turner, Kirkwood | King, William x | Harrison, Wm., son of Henry |
| Hardesty, Joseph Jnr. | Turner, Alexander x | Charlton, Thomas x |
| Mackall, Thomas | Stallings, William x | Irny, [?] John x |
| Gibson, John | Stallings, John x | Duckett, John |
| Lyon, James | Brassan, John x | Machoy, Robert [Mackay?] |
| Spicknall, Basil x | Lattimer [?] Joseph, Esq. | |

Calvert County, Ss. I hereby certify that the Several persons whose names are hereunto annexed did take, Repeat and Subscribe the Oath to their names prefixed in my presence, pursuant to the Act of General Assembly of this State entitled An Act for the better Security of the Government. Witness my Hand this 2d day of March, 1778.

CHARLES GRAHAME.

A list of persons fined in Capt. James Graham's Company for non attendance in Battalion 15th Sept., 1777.

| | |
|---|---|
| Scott, Wm. | £1, 10 |
| Trott, Saml. | 1, 10 |
| Deale, Richard | 1, 10 |
| Scrivener, Richard | 1, 10 |
| Whittington, John | 1, 10 |
| Trott, Saml. (of Thos.) | 1, 10 |
| | £9, 0 |

Persons fined in Capt. Graham's Company for non attendance in Battalion in Nov., 1777.

| | |
|---|---|
| Hardesty, Elisha | £1, 10 |
| Weems, David | 1, 10 |
| Leach, Benj. | 1, 10 |
| Hardesty, Thomas | 1, 10 |
| Howey, ——— | 1, 10 |
| Hinton, Richard, Junr. | 1, 10 |
| Scrivenor, Richard, | 1, 10 |
| Whittington, John Junr. | 1, 10 |
| Eades, Jacob | 1, 10 |
| Newell, Wm. | 1, 10 |
| Freeman, Saml. | 1, 10 |

| | |
|---|---|
| Marshall, Martin | 1, 10 |
| Weems, James (of David) | 1, 10 |
| Piles, Leonard | 1, 10 |
| Scears, John Junr. | 1, 10 |
| Trott, Saml., (of Thos.) | 1, 10 |
| Cowman, Joseph | 1, 10 |
| Scott, Wm. | 1, 10 |
| Trott, Saml. | 1, 10 |
| Deele, Richard | 1, 10 |
| Marshall, Henry | 1, 10 |
| Stephens, Wm. | 1, 10 |
| Stone, Wm. | 1, 10 |
| Turner, Wm. Junr. | 1, 10 |
| Hinton, Richard | 1, 10 |
| Whittington, Samuel | 1, 10 |
| Brown, James | 1, 10 |
| King, John Junr. | 1, 10 |
| | £42, 0 |

Ireland, Thomas .............. 1, 10
Wilkinson, Joseph, Co. 8.

The within is a true copy taken from the Return made by Co. 8, Joseph Wilkinson.

Benj.: Meckall —th [probably oath].
Lt. Calvt. County.

* Original presented to the Columbia Historical Society March 20, 1917, by Miss Sallie Summervell Mackall, Washington, D. C. Permission to publish is kindly granted by the said society through its President and Secretary.

"x" after the names means "His mark," in the original record.

# INDEX

The numbers refer to pages, excepting that numbers in parentheses, "(3)," indicate frequency of appearance of the name upon the indicated page; and numbers in parallel marks, "|3|," indicate the number given to the name upon the indicated page.

40

seph, 3 |4|; Joseph Belt, 7
|82|; Joshua, 25 (3), 26, 27
(6), 29 (4), 30 (4), 31 (3),
32 (6), 33 (2), 34 (3), 35
(6), 36 (4); Josiah, 9
|103|, 31; Jos.as, 28, 29;
Lawson, 4 |331|; Leven, 6
|19|; Menum, 3 |113|; Nin.
6 |3|; Ninian, 22; Ninian
Edmonston, 3 |30|; Patrick,
26, 28; Richard, 7 |64|, 30,
32; Robert, 3 |112|, 3 |18|,
7 |58|, son of N. 7 |14|,
Robert Asa, 3 |165|; Saml.
4 |239|, Jr. 7 |31|; Thadous,
7 |20|; Theodore, 35; Thos.
7 |69|, 7 |18|, 30, of Geo.
6 |15|, of Ninian, 34; Wal-
ter, 3 |101|; Wm. Dent, 36;
Zachariah, 8 |110|; Zeph-
aniah, 3 |7|, 3 |173|, 6 |2|.
Beamer, Henry, 22.
Bean, Beane, Been, Geo. 31,
33, 34; Henry, 18 |8|, John
16 |14|, 16 |148|, 18 |9|.
Beanes, Beans, Christopher,
5 |49|; Wm. 22, 26, 27.
Beard, David, 17 |44|.
Beatty, Mark, 20 |8|; Wm. 22.
Beck, James, 26, 27, 28 (2),
29 (3), 30 (3), 31 (2), 33,
34, 35 (2).
Beckett, James, 22; Wm. 22
(2).
Beckwith, Basil, 5 |107|; John
5 |88|; Wm. 5 |93|.
Becraft, Abm. 24; Benj. 24,
Jr. 8 |35|; Geo. Jr. 24; John
24; Peter 24 (2).
Bedds, Absalom, 4 |287|;
James, 4 |327|.
Belt, Benj. 34; Humphrey,
26, 27; James, 35; Middle-
ton, 34; Thos. 4 |237|, 31.
Beezley, Mosses, 7 |82|.
Beggezley, Benj. 3 |5|.
Beggs, 12 |22|.
Begold, Wm. 24.
Beiraft, Peter 8 |5|.
Be'l,—see Beall.
Belser, Peter, 22.
Belt, Benoni, 14 |140|; Carl-
ton, 9 |47|; Higginson 10
|134|; John, 2 |14|; Joseph
8 |4|; Joseph Sprigg, 7 |4|.
Beltzhoover, Melchor, 20 |13|.
Bence, Geo. 26.
Benedict, Bowman, 20 |2|.
Benjamin. Abraham. 5 |55|.
Benson, Wm. 2 |89|.
Benton, Benj. S. 8 |83|; Jo-
seph, 8 |28|; Wm. 8 |93|.
Benwick, Wm. 14 |70|.
Beresford, John, 17 |22|.
Bergd, Peter, 17 |20|.
Berger, John, 22.
Bernard, Jacob, 2 |35|.
Bernth. Jacob, 19 |199|.
Berry, Bassel, 14 |166|; Benj.
32, 33, 34; Elisha, 26, 28,

31; Jeremiah, 3 |119|; John,
3 |118|; Nicholas, 3 |29|;
Richard, 3 |35|; William,
26, 27 (4), 29 (3), 30 (4),
31 (2), 33 (4), 34 (2), 35
(2), 36; Zachariah, 30, 32,
36.
Besty, Wm. 17 |23|.
Betts, Higginson, 2 |151|.
Beven, Leonard, 17 |64|.
Bigg, John, 3 |184|.
Biggs, Samuel, 9 |37|.
B.gnell, Robert, 8 |36|.
Billmyer, Leonard, 13 |21|.
Bilmore, John, 17 |13|.
Bird, Francis, 31, 33, 34.
Birdwhistle, Thos. 2 |11|.
Bisbin, James, 9 |90|.
Biscoe, Bennett, 21.
Bishop, Jacob, Plates, III, IV.
Blacher, Fredk. 17 |11|.
Black, John 18 |10|; Saml. 19
|26|; Wm. 19 |27|.
Blacklock, Richd. 8 |29|; Thos.
34; Junior, 31; Nicholas,
33, 34, 35 (2).
Blackmore, Calep, 17 |62|;
Wm. 17 |56|, 6 |42|.
Blackwood, Wm. 4 |322|.
Bladen, Thos. 4 |362|.
Blair, Wm. 22.
Blanford, Thos. 27.
Blany, Col. 23.
Bleny, Rudolph, 19 |59|.
Blew, Abraham, 16 |91|.
Blowers, Benj. 3 |205|.
Bloyss, David, 7 |70|.
Bluebaug, Jacob, 22.
Blume, Henry 17 |4|.
Boardon, John 7 |60|.
Bockes, John, 22.
Boerhaane, Valentine 8 |33|.
Boerhaave, Simon 9 |107|.
Bogler, John 7 |54|.
Bohrer, Geo. 13 |29|.
Bolsom, Thos. 5 |430|.
Bonham, Peter, 16 |22|.
Bonifant, James, 27, 28, 35,
36.
Bonman, Simon, 19 |50|.
Bonnett, John, 16 |25|.
Boogher, Andrew, 22.
Boond, John, 17 |16|.
Boone, Abrum, 22; Alexis, 33,
34; Electus, 35; Francis,
28, 35; Francis, son Henry,
31.
Bordam, Jacob, 19 |113|.
Boreman, Geo. 3 |208|.
Rorman, Jacob, 4 |372|.
Bosse, David, 14 |175|.
Bosswell, James, 4 |223|; Nic-
holas, 4 |217|.
Boteler, Chas. 33, 34; Edwd.
25; Lingan, 33; Thos. 26,
28; Thos. of Chas. 33.
Botts. Andrew 17 |8|.
Boucher, Rev. Jonathan, 29.
Boughslough, Peter, 17 |96|.
Bounds, Thos. 22 (2).
Bousser, John 19 |182|.

Bouttauff, Andrew, 17 |34|;
Martin, 17 |36|.
Bowen, Chas. 15 |49|; Fredk.
15 |50|, 19 |90|; John 9 |54|.
Bower, Abraham, 20 |236|;
Frederick, 14 |151|; George
17 |5|; Jacob, 21 |58|; Mau-
rice, 20 |240|; Morris 17
|2|.
Bowie, Allen, 7 |67|; Fielder,
25 (2), 26, 27 (2), 28, 29
(3), 30 (4), 31, 32 (4), 33
(2), 34 (2), 35 (2); Wm.
22; Wm. (3d), 25, 29, 30,
32, 33, 34; Wm. Sprigg, 30.
Bowling, John, 27, 28, 31, 33,
34.
Bowman, Aron, 19 |20|; Dan.
14 |58|; Jacob, 19 |85|;
John, 19 |18|, 22; Sterling,
14 |57|.
Boyall, Wm. 4.
Boyd, Abraham, 6 |146|, 27,
30 (4), 31 (2), 32 (2), 33
(3), 34 (2), 35(4), 36 (2);
Archibald, 34; John, 6
|138|; Leroy S. 25; Robert
37; Thos. 25, 26, 27 (3), 28
(2), 29 (3), 30 (3), 31 (2),
32 (3), 33 (3), 34 (2), 35
(3), 36 (2); Walter, 15
|34|, |35|; Wm. Sr. 20 |14|;
Wm. 6 |136|, 16 |34|.
Bracco, John, 22.
Brackaunier, Peter, 20 |251|.
Bradford, Wm. 13 |19|.
Bradshear, Wm. Jr. 24.
Bragg, Wm. 6.
Brand, James, 13 |34|; James,
Jr. 14 |49|.
Brandenburgh, Christopher
12 |40|.
Brandish, Thos. 9 |79|.
Brandstatter, Andrew, 20
|238|.
Branner, Philip 19 |6|.
Branon, Patrick, 21 |101|.
Braselton, Isaac, 24 |5|.
Brashears, Jeremiah, 28;
John, son of John, 27; Jo-
seph, 26, 28, 35; Morris, 3
|84|, Morris, Jr. 3 |86|;
Nacey, 31; Thos. 28.
Brassan, John 37 |2|.
Brather, Rignal, 19 |144|.
Braudsaburgh, Saml. 22.
Bray, Henry, 16 |30|.
Breeze, Andrew, 16 |23|.
Bremick, Daniel, 13 |32|.
Brendlinges, Conrad, 17 |9|.
Bresh, Philip, 20 |227|.
Brice, James, 22.
Bright, Geo. 14 |89|.
Brightwell, Richd., 26, 27, 31
(2), 33 (2), 34.
Briscoe, Gerrard, 1, 2; Robert,
2 |142|.
Britain, States, 37.
Brnond, Burdet Gray, 2 |141|.
Broadack. Joseph. 6 |69|.
Broadback, Henry, 22.

## F

Fackler, Michael, 20 |262|.
Fage, John, 17 |46|.
Fahrman, Henry, 19 |169|.
Fair, Francis, 17 |43|.
Falconer, Gilbert, 22, 27.
Fallows, Wm. 12 |4|.
Fardo, John Lewis, 8 |87|.
Faris, John, 23.
Farmer, Henry, 13 |36|; John, 5 |80|; Saml. 14 |83|; Wm. 3 |124|.
Farmwold, L., 23.
Farrall, Farrel, Ferrell, 4 |240|; John, 7 |98|; Thos. 14 |114|.
Faughman, John, 23.
Faur, Henry, 20 |9|.
Faut, Banet, 15 |31|.
Feaild, Thos. 16 |38|.
Fear, Geo. 17 |125|.
Feigety, Peter, 19 |83|.
Fellows, Richard, 24.
Fenemore, Wm. 9 |7|.
Fenwick, Ignatius, 32.
Fergusson, John, 25; Wm. 31, 33, 34.—See Forgerson, Furguson.
Fernhaver, John Chris, 24.
Ferrel, James, 3 |181|; John, 3 |179|.
Ferver, Fervor, Leonard & Philip, 23.
Fethworth, Isaac, 16 |85|.
Fetherkeyl, Geo. Michael, 9 |104|.
Fetzer, Philip, 19 |135|.
F'ckus, Chas. 24.
Fields, Abraham, 2 |71|; John, 6 |60|; Joseph, 4 |400|; Mathew, 2 |128|.
Fiery, Joseph 16 |26|.
Fife, Abijah, 6 |78|.
Figeby, John, 19 |34|.
Fight, John, 15 |51|.
Fightmaster, Geo. 4 |318|; John, 4 |316|.
Filman, Mathias, 17 |49|.
Findlay, Robt., 29.
Finnesee, Wm., 23.
Fish, Robt., 33.
Fisher, Adam, 17 |38|; Abraham 19 |205|; Daniel, 19 |74|; Jacob, 20 |10|, 21 |86|; John, 21 |85|; Martin, 5 |46|.
Fitch, James, 13 |68|; Joseph, 17 |45|.
Fitzgerreld, etc., Edward, 3 |102|; Mathew, 3 |103|; Richd. 3 |28|; Walter, 4 |348|; Wm. 3 |12|.
Fitzhugh, Peregne, 37.
Fivecoats, Michael, 17 |93|.
Flack, Fleck, James, 21 |72|; John, 12 |30|.
Flegle, Chas., 23.
Fleming, James, 7 |33|; John, 7 |24|, Jr. 7 |44|.
Flennard, John Jr., 19 |29|; Rudolph, 19 |189|.

Fletcher, Thomas, 9 |104|.
Fleunard, John, 20 |269|.
Flick, Adam, 13 |84|; John, 14 |15|; Wm. 13 |67|.
Fligh, Nal., 23.
Flint, John, 18 |26|; Joseph, 18 |25|; Thos. 8 |4|.
Flock, Jacob, 16 |133|.
Flora, James, 18 |28|; John, 18 |27|.
Floskinson, Hugh, 10 |31|.
Flower, Robert, 16 |106|.
Flying Camp, 36.
Foard, Henry, 17 |49|; James 17 |57|; Robert, 17 |48|; Wm. Jr., 27, 28, 31, 33, 34.
Focpeh, George, 16 |139|.
Foeach, Danl. 23.
Foglesong, Geo., 23.
Fonter, John, 13 |11|.
Forbes, James, 22.
Forguson, Forgresong, Christian, 17 |44|; Samuel, 16 |36|.
Forman, John & Jacob, 23.
Forset, James, 3 |42|.
Forster, Luke, 19 |8|; Ralph, 25 (2), 28.
Forwhoaler, Frans, 7 |15|.
Foulton, Robt. 8 |62|.
Fower, James, 16 |104|.
Fowler, Elisha, 9 |81|.
Fox, Frederick, 13 |42|; Geo. 13 |33|.
Frants, Stofel, 14 |201|.
Frazer, Jonthn., 23; Thos. 23.
Frederick Co., Md., 12, 22, 24; Hundred, 18.
Freeman, Richd., 6 |91|; Saml. 37.
Frend, Cacob, 17 |47|.
Fr'ddle, John, 23.
Frisel, Jacob, 14 |202|.
Fruth, Martin, 19 |47|.
Frye, Abrm. and Isaac, 23.
Fryer, Richd. 2 |59|.
Fulconar, Alexander, 13 |18|.
Funk, Jacob & John, 12 |37 & 38|.
Furguson, John, Sr. 14 |35|; Joseph, 9 |29|—See Ferguson.
Fve, Wm. 17 |48|.
Fyffe, James, Sr. 10 |159|, James 11 |185|; Jonathan, 11 |189|; Joseph, 10 |128|.

## G

Gable, Phillips, 17 |51|.
Gabral, Abraham, 19 |183|; John, 15 |33|.
Gairing, Christopher, 17 |55|.
Gaither, Basil, 2 |10|; Benj. 4 |385|, 31; Burgess, 5 |44|; Edward, Sr. 13 |44|; Eliiah 11 |85|; Ephrain, 3 |203|; Henry, 3 |54|, 12 |2|; John, 3 |116|, 13 |45|; Nicholas, 2 |129|; Richard, 12 |32|; Vechel, 14 |91|; Wm. 3 |64|.

Gale, Levin, 22.
Gall, George, 16 |5|.
Gandy, Jacob, 24.
Gantt, Erasmus, 11 |20|; Geo. 31, 33, 34; John M. 11 |19|; Levi, 29; Thos. 30, 32; Jr. 25 (2), 26, 27 (2), 28, 29 (2), 31, 34.
Gardiner, Gardinour, Clement, 35; Francis, 17 |57|; Jacob, 14 |20|; James, 11 |42|.
Garlock, Garlick, John, 18 |32|; Joseph, 8 |46|.
Garner, Clement, 35; Paul, 9 |88|.
Garrett, Garrott, Barton, 23; Edward, 3 |153|; John, 23.
Gartrell, Aaron, 3 |194|; Chas. 3 |87|; Francis, 4 |247|; Jehoshaphat, 4 |213|; Joseph, 3 |41|; Rich. 3 |40|.
Gashell, Thos, 4 |291|.
Gassler, Anthony, 8 |26|.
Gastrell, Francis 3 |20|; John, 3 |21|.
Gates, Geats, Edwd. 3 |180|; James, 9 |98|.
Gatton, Azariah, 27; Benj. 9 |89|; James, 9 |49|; Richd. 6 |147|; Wm. 6 |144|; Zackariah, 6 |148|.
Gayrherd, John, 20 |228|.
Gazaway, Chas. 6 |37|.
Gee, David, 4 |295|.
Gel, John Baptist, 4 |216|.
Gentle, George, 4 |403|.
George, Joseph, 21 |59|; Saml. 18 |30|; Thos. 20 |11|.
Gerlock, Henry, 16 |24|.
Gettings, Gittings, Basil, 7 |21|; Benj. 7 |12|, 8 |122|; Henry, 2 |125|; James, 22.
Gibbs, John Harrison, 34.
Gibhart, John, 8 |16|.
Gibler, Jacob, 19 |62|.
Gibson, James, 37; John, 11 |190|, 37; Richd. 37.
Gilbert, John 16 |29|; Michael, 18 |31|.
Gilhart, |Gibhart?|, Christopher, 18 |162|.
Gilksy, Saml. 6 |11|.
Gillespie, David, 17 |56|; Francis, 14 |188|; Geo. 16 |2|; James, 12 |27|; John, 18 |29|; Thos. 16 |22|.
Gillham, John, 4 |401|; Thos. 9 |57|.
Gilpin, Francis Green, 14 |92|.
Gladhill, Wm. 13 |33|.
Glasner, John, 15 |15|.
Glass, Michael, 19 |200|.
Glaze, Glase, Gla?s, Basil, 4 |313|; Joseph, 8 |67|; Nathan, 4 |383|; Nathaniel, 3 |182|; Saml. 3 |158|; Wm. 7 |91|.
Gobbel, Geo. 24 |8|.

Macdougle, John, 3 |188|; Saml. 3 |189|.
Macgill, John, 30; Thos. 26, 27 (2), 28 (2), 29 (2), 20 (4), 31, 32 (3).
Machoy or Mackay (?), Robert, 37.
Mack, Jacob, 13 |3|.
Mackall, Benj., 22, 37; Benj. 4th, 22; Sallie Summerville, 37; Thos., 37.
Mackebee, James, 8 |100|.
Mackelfresh, David, 3 |58|; John, 3 |61|; Richd. 3 |59| & |68|.
Mackenzie, Aaron, 15 |19|; Daniel, 15 |37|; Gabriel, 15 |18|; Saml. 15 |30|.
Macnabb, John, 12 |3|.
Maconkey, Jacob, 19 |54|; John, 19 |55|.
Macsgemer, John 13 |36|.
Maddin, Maddon, Fred 23; John, 10 |71|; Jonathan, Jnr. 10 |67|; Jonathan Snr. 10 |68|; Mordica, 20 |40|; Richd. 10 |70|.
Maddocks, Maddox, Chas. 30, 32 (2), 35 (2), 36; Thos. 8 |69|.
Magrath, William, 9 |74|.
Magruder, Alex. Howard, 25, 26, 27 (3), 28, 29 (3), 30 (3), 31 (2), 32 (3), 34 (2), 36; Archibald, 8 |119|; (3), 31 (2), 32 (3), 34 (2), Caleb C. Jr., 11, 25; Edward, 8 |81|, 32; Elias, 8 |12|; Enoch, 8 |37|, 22; George, 11 |30|; Geo. Fraser, 28; Haswell, 26, 28, 31; Henderson, 34; Hezekiah, 8 |13|; Isaac, 5 |95|; James, 10 |80|, James Jr. 23; Jeremiah, 25(2), 26, 27; John, 8 |121|, 23; John B. 5 |13|; John Read, 25 (2), 26 (2), 27 (2), 28 (2), 29 (3), 30 (3), 31 (2), 32 (4), 33 \2), 34, 35 (3), 36; Joseph, 7 |2|; Josiah, 8 |23|; Levin 8 |2|; Nathan, 5 |90|; Nathaniel, 8 |9|, |135|, 22; Ninian, 8 |57|; Ninian Beall, 8 |109|; Norman Bruce, 8 |33|; Patrick, 11 |9|; Richd. 8 |88|; Samuel 3d. 8 |41|; Saml. B. 8 |71|; Saml. Brewer, 8 |35|; Saml. W. 8 |1|; Walter. 8 |126|; Wm. Beall. 8 |22|; Wm. Offutt, 8 |25|; Zaak, 5 |10|; Zachariah, 8 |13|; Zadok, 22; Warehouse, 28.
Maguire, Andrew, 7 |7|.
Mahniger, Henry, 20 |213|.
Maholl, Samuel, 8 |80|; Stephen, 8 |59|.
Mahoney, Henry, 14 |63|; Thos. 14 |27|.
Makillip, Henry, 19 |41|.

Malcome, James, 17 |107|.
Malone, Thomas 2 |54|.
Malott, Thomas, 14 |102|.
Man (Maw), Charles, 33.
Mandel, Christian, 20 |19|.
Mandey, Balthasar, 19 |126|.
Manley, John, 26, 28, 31, 33, 34.
Manning, James, 9 |91|.
Mantz, Peter, 23.
Maquess, John, 6 |133|.
Marbury, Luke, 25, 26, 27, 29, 31, 32.
Mardon, James, 7 |63|; John, 7 |57|.
Marker, M chael, 13 |35|.
Markwell, George, 16 |87|.
Marshall, Geo. 23 (2); Henry, 37; James, 7 |28|; Martin, 37; Richd. 34.
Marsner, Joseph, 15 |81|.
Martin, James, 14 |16|; Joseph, 18 |54|; Lenox, 11 |27|; Luther, 11 |8|, 30; Nehemiah, 16 |26|; Robert, 17 |92|; Saml. 6 |36|; Wm. 18 |50|, |55|.
Maryland Historical Society, Pref., 1, 24.
Maryland Records, etc. 22.
Mason, Alexander, 4 |343|; Jonathan, 3 |191|, 24; Richard, 4 |281|.
Mathew, Conrad, 23.
Mathews, Jacob, 23; John, 23; Philip, 23; Wm. 17 |109|.
Mattingly, Barnet, 15 |24|; Henry, 15 |66|; Joseph, 15 |11|; Richd. 15 |9|.
Maxfield, James, 22.
Mayes, Andrey, 17 |120|.
Meckall—See Mackall.
Medley, William, 5 |79|.
Meek, Meeks, David, 15 |32|; Geo. 11 |172|; Thos. 19 |179|.
Meezes, Valentine, 3 |14|.
Melot, Melott, Benj. 14 |183|; Joseph, 13 |22|.
Melton, James, 23.
Mengennor, John, 17 |93|.
Messersmith, Andrew, 14 |146|; Wallintine, 17 |88|.
Metcalf, Edward, 4 |376|; Thos. 24; Wm. 14 |73|.
Meyer, Adam, 13 |79|; Felia, 20 |232|; Geo. 13 |72|; Jacob, 13 |78|; Lodwick, 13 |47|; Michl. Snr. 13 |16|; Peter, 13 |75|.
Michill, Benj. 10 |136|; John, 16 |55|; John Everhart, 15 |12|; Ludwick, 14 |24|; Morrice 3 |49|; Robt. 10 |92|; Thos. 3 |91|.
Middle Battalion, 36.
Middogh, John, 9 |97|.
Midolealf, John, 13 |36|.
Mifford, James, 23.
Mikesell, Andrew, 23

Miles, John, 9 |84|; Thos. 8 |129|.
Miller, Adam, 16 |15|, 23; Anthony, 23; Christian, 13 |23|; Conrad, 15 |54|, 23; Daniel, 15 |53|, 23; David, 13 |85|; Fredk. 18 |95|; Geo. 18 |96|, 19 |148|; Hans, 19 |82|; Henry 19 |31|; Henry of Conrad, 19 |203|; Henry of Hans, 19 |202|; Jacob, 15 |52|; John 14 |142|, 18 |99|, 19 |196|, 20 |264|; John Solomon, 14 |79|; Luds, 23; Michl. 23, 19 |168|; Nicholas, 24; Solomon, 17 |91|; Thos. 10 |86|; Ulrick, 17 |90|; Wm. 14 |67|, 21 |65|, 23.
Millhouse, John, 17 |83|.
Millme, John, 18 |57|.
Mills, Chas. 23; Jacob, 18 |52|; James, 18 |53|; Jesse 6 |43|.
Mizers, Valentine, 3 |23|.
Mcale, John, 22.
Moberly, Mobberly, John & Lewis, 24.
Mobley, Archibald, 4 |270|.
Mock, Peter, 17 |89|.
Mockabey, Mockbee, Mockebee, Mockeby, Brock, 3 |131|; John, 6 |20|; Joseph, 33; Zacha, 7 |80|; Zepha, 7 |85|.
Moffet, William, 18 |94|.
Mogemer, Lodowick, 13 |32|.
Molett, John, 14 |117|; Peter, 14 |97|; Theodore, 14 |100|.
Momoughan, John, 19 |204|.
Mong, Adam, 21 |88|.
Mony (?), Adam Jr., 12 |14|; Nicholas, 21 |89|.
Monohon, Thomas, 24.
Monroe, Barney, 12 |11|.
Montgomery Co., Md., 1-11.
Moodie, William, 31, 33 (2), 34.
Mooll, Henry, 20 |256|.
Moone, William, 8 |43|.
Moonehead, Joseph, 13 |20|.
Moor, Moore, Barton, 8 |76|; Christopher, 17 |99|; Elisha, 8 |47|; Geo. 13 |30|; James, 6 |84|, 8 |26|; John 14 |147|; John Wm. 3 |80|; Joseph 17 |70|; Mordica, 4 |276|; Philip, 16 |18|; Saml. 3 |85|; Silvanus, 3 |105|; Thos. 3 |200|; Wm. 16 |108|—Abram, Jr. 24; Geo. 32; Geo. Jr. 35; James, 27 (2), 29; John 23; Wm. 30.
Morford, Daniel, 17 |85|.
Morgan, Nathaniel, 20 |37|.
Morison, Joseph, 14 |21|.
Morton, William, 26, 28, 33, 34.
Moss, Francis, 8 |11|; Robert, 9 |67|.

|20|; Nicholas, 9 |99|; Wm. 18 |103|.
Peach, James, 6 |158|.
Peack, Peek, Peck, Benj., 5 |37|; Geo. 13 |23|, 17 |46|; Lewis, 5 |29|; Thos. 5 |5|.
Pearce, Pierce, Benj. 18 |61|; Benj. Notley, 9 |83|; James, 22; Thos. 31, 34; Wm. 26.
Pearie, Pearre, Perrie James, 35, 36; John 26, 28, PeDeeomtz (PeDecomtz?), Nicholas, 9 |40|.
Peddicort, Nathan, 14 |115|, |186|.
Peen, Benj. 3 |128|, |190|; Benj. Davis, 3 |140|; Edwd. 3 |135|; John 4 |251|.
Peer, Peere, John Baptist, 4 |341|; Philip, 24.
Peifer, Martin, 19 |4|.
Pelly, Harrison, 5 |465|; James, 6 |83|.
Pence, Jacob, 18 |105|.
Pendleberry, Marmaduke, 4 |265|.
Penny, Joseph, 4 |395|.
Perey, Perry, Chas. 6 |161|; Danl. 12 |18|; Erasmus, 3 |174|; James, 3 |137|, 5 |105, 11 |21|, 35; John, 5 |424|; Joseph 3 |115|, 20 |21|; Joshua, 6 |442|.
Peter, Baltksor, 15 |22|; Michael, 14 |108|; Robert 9 |64|, Jr. 8 |48|.
Peterson, Henry, 24.
Petters, Abraham, 16 |101|.
Petry, Jacob, 19 |107|.
Pflenger, Pfleuger, Leonard, 19 |88|; Peter, 20 |259|.
Phelps, John, Senr. |13 |29|, Jr. 13 |40|.
Philpott, Barton, 23.
Phillips, Thomas, 18 |60|.
Pickenbaugh, Geo. Lo., 23.
Pierce—See Pearce.
Pifer, Manuell, 20 |22|.
Pigman, Mathew, 3 |50|; Nathaniel, 3 |77|.
Piles, Francis, 26; Leonard, 37.
Pinchback, John, 2 |13|.
Pindle. Jacob, 18 |63|.
Pine. James, 19 |176|.
Pinkley, Jacob, 20 |23|.
Piper, Jacob, 13 |80|; Leonard, 15 |3|.
Pitcach, Benj. 18 |66|.
Placker, Samuel, 13 |38|.
Plummer, Jeremiah, 10 |16|; John. 15 |70|; Philliman, 3 |57|: Thos. 15 |45|, 28.
Poch, Phillip, 3 |109|.
Poens, David, 15 |10|.
Pofsenbargor, John, 13 |76|; Valentine. 13 |82|.
Polhower, Sand. 23.
Poole. Henry, 24; Joseph, 10 |12|: Thos., 37.
Pope, Nathaniel, 31, 34.

Porter, Henry, 15 |38|.
Porterfield, James, 4 |269|.
Post, Val. 23.
Postle, Saml., 18 |62|.
Poston, Saml. 31, 33.
Postlethwort, Wm. 16 |123|.
Poth, Michael, 20 |241|.
Potter, Nathaniel, 22.
Potterof, Casper, 15 |26|.
Pottinger, John, 14 |116|.
Potts, Jonathan, 18 |64|; Saml. 18 |65|.
Powell, Nathan, 20 |7|.
Power, Benj. 16 |114|; Edwd. 13 |57|; Nicholas, 10 |155|.
Prater, Prather, Aaron, 5 |94|; Azariah, 5 |97|; Baruch, 7 |46|; Basil, 17 |51|; Benj. 4 |356|, 32; Chas. 16 |102|; James 16 |121|; John, 4 |286|; Nathan, 29; Richard, 16 |27|; Thos. 13 |25|; 17 |55|; Walter, 6 |139|; Zaccai, 6 |140|.
Preast, Henry, 8 |70|.
Price, Ignatius, 26, 28; Josiah, 20 |41|; Richd. 8 |120|; Thos. 33.
Prigmore, Jonathan, 14 |101|; Theodores, 14 |98|, |99|.
Prince George's Co., Md., 11, 25.
Pritchett, Chas. 6 |127|; Elias, 7 |79|; Wm. 5, |47|.
Proheth, William 14 |192|.
Prue, Joseph, 18 |104|.
Pry, John, 17 |41|.
Pullen, William, 20 |5|.
Purdey, Purdy, Chas. 9 |60|; Richd. 10 |158|.
Purdom, John, 4 |371|.
Purnell, Thos. of John, 22.
Purse¹, Pursell, Daniel, 16 |135|; David. 16 |157|; John, 16 |138|; Thos. 16 |136|.

### Q.

Queen, Elisha 26; Joseph, 34; Richd. 26, 28, 30; Walter, 27, 28; Wm. 23.
Queen Anne Warehouse, 28.
Quick. Aaron, 16 |18|, |31|; Andrew, 16 |20|; Benj. 16 |21|; Dennis, 16 |15|; Jacob, 16 |17|; Thos. 16 |16|
Quinn, George, 20 |39|.
Quordren, John, 3 |127|.

### R.

Ragan, John, 19 |7|.
Ramsey, Wm. 23.
Ranaday, Chas. 16 |81|; John. 16 |5|.
Randell. John, 5 |98|.
Rapp, Matthias, 19 |155|.
Rashr, Wm. 16 |9|.
Ratles, Francis, 4 |292|.
Raughly, Geo. 17 |89|.
Rawlings, John, 2 |41|.

Ray, Benj. 6 |9|; James, 8 |73|, 33; John, Jr., 2 |9|; Nicholas, 4 |253|; Thos. 8 |51|; Wm. 4 |51|, 10 |14|, 16 |86|, 27, 29 (2), 30.
Raymer, John, 19 |158|.
Rayon, John, 9 |83|.
Read, Reed, Geo. 7 |24|; John, 6 |5|; Jonathan, 10 |17|; Joseph, 16 |117|; Mathew, 10 |18|; Richd., 18 |69|; Saml. 17 |119|, 21 |95|; Thos. 2 |32|; Wm. 13 |22|.
Roader, Reeder, John, 21; Mike, 24; Simon 10 |29|.
Reese, Andr. & Fred, 23.
Refneh, Casper, 18 |111|.
Rehb, John, 19 |48|.
Reichel, Adam, 19 |86|.
Reiley—See Riley.
Reinhart, Geo. 19 |97|.
Reinhold, Fittus, 20 |224|.
Reintzel, Reintzel, Anthy. 23; Daniel 8 |34|; Jacob, 6 |134|.
Reips, John, 16 |30|.
Reisner, Jacob, 9 |110|.
Reitzel, Valentine, 8 |17|.
Remington, John. 7 |39|.
Rench, Rentch, Andrew, 20, 22.
Rennolds—See Reynolds.
Replogle, Philop, 16 |6|.
Rerls, Frederick, 17 |86|.
Returns, Justice of Peace—Barnes, John, 16; Barrits, Saml. 16; Briscoe, Gerrard, 1, 2; Bruce. Andrew, 15; Burgess, Edwd. 3-5; Campbell, Oneas, 9, Officer, 11; Chaplin, Joseph. 14; Cellar, John, 15; Cruso, Chrs. 12; Davis, Richd. 13; Deakins, Wm. 1, Jnr. 6; Hughs, Saml. 12; Hutts, James, 9; Jones, Chas. 7; Magruder, Saml. W. 8; Offutt, Joseph 7, 11; Rentch, Andrew, 20; Schneblev, Henry, 19; Sprigg, Joseph, 20; Stull. John, 17; Thompson, Richd. 8; Williams, Elisha, 10; Wilson, Joseph 5, 11; Wootton, Thos. Sprigg, 10; Yates, Wm. 18.
Reuh, Mathias, 21 |68|.
Reymer, Frederick, 19 |127|.
Revnolds, Rennolds, Chas. 3 |90|, 7 |37|: Edward, 22; Francis. 13 |14|; Jeremiah. 14 |176|, John, 13 |5|, 14 |36|: Joseph of John, 13 |2|. Joseph 14 |10|; Wm. 6 |33|.
Reyos. John, 3 |66|.
Rhoades. Roades, Jacob, 5 |72|. 23; John, 5 |76|; Wm. 14 |155|.

Rice, Andrew 15 |46|; Nicholas, 21 |70|.
Richards, Ritchards, Geo. Hall, 16 |14|; John 5 |421|; Leonard, 4 |411|.
Richardson, Geo., 15 |20|; Thos. 26, 27.
Richmond, John, 37.
Rickenbach, ——, 19 |197|.
Ricker, Peter, 23.
Ricketts, Anthony, 2 |106|; Benj. 5 |58|, |441|; Jacob, 5 |108|; Joseph 4 |212|; Mezchant, 3 |17|; Richard, 3 |202|; Thos. 6 |162|; Wm. 4 |243|.
Richold, Maynard, 18 |67|.
Rictenawer, Peter, 20 |273|.
Rietenower, Rietenower, Ridenow, Ridenower, etc., David, 19 |52|; Geo. 20 |235|; Henry, 19 |14|, |46|, |201|; Jacob, 15 |24|, 19 |117|; Ludwick, 15 |27|; Martin 20 |24|, |233|; Matthias, 19 |186|, 20 |26|; Nicholas, 19 |37|, |105|.
Ridgely, Fredk. 20 |47|; H. Jr. 11 |12|; Isaac, 13 |38|.
Ridgeway, Ridgway, Ridgerway, etc., Isaac, 8 |116|; Masum, 3 |44|; Robert 4 |370|; Wm. 3 |38|.
Rieffenach, Philip 20 |221|.
Rientzel, Reintzel, Andrew, 5 |106|, 11 |41|.
Rigby, Nathaniel, 22.
Rigden, Thomas, 8 |7|.
Rigger, Casper, 20 |217|; John 20 |216|; Peter, 21 |75|.
Riggs, Azeriah, 9 |81|; Benj. 9 |82|; John, 4 |218|, 10 |61|; Saml. 3 |62|; Thos. 4 |235|; Thos. Wheelen, 9 |80|.
Rigney, Terice, 4 |404|.
Right, Saml. 16 |71|.
Riley, Reiley, Hugh, 8 |27|; James, 2 |34|; Jeremiah, 2 |40| 26, 28; John, 12 |31|; Johnson Michael, 28, 29, 30 (2), 32 (2), 35, 36; Ninian, 8 |8|; Zachariah, 2 |122|.
Rimill, Phillip 20 |26|.
Rinehart, Thomas, 20 |11|.
Riner, George, 23.
Ringgold, Wm. Jun. 22.
Ritchinson, Wm. 5 |420|.
Ritter, Elias, 19 |101|; Jacob. 19 |100|.
Roadbush, Daniel, 23.
Roberson, Nathan. 7 |88|.
Roberts, Bas'l. 5 |83|; Ezekiah, 2 |66|; James, 10 |154|; John, 23: Richard, 6 |73|; Wm. 14 |17|; Zephaniah, 10 |145|.
Robertson, Geo. 5 |472|;

James, 11 |210|; John, 10 |122|; Wm. 6 |165|.
Robie, Roby, Benj. 14 |158|; Berry, 3 |144|; Ignatius, 4 |416|; John Tayler, 9 |101|; Lawrance, 14 |121|; Michael, 13 |39|; Owen, 14 |164|; Thomas 14 |87|; Wm. 14 |109|.
Robinson, John, 33; Leonard, 5 |429|.
Rockenback, Jacob, 13 |77|.
Rogers, John, 30, 31, 33, 34, 35.
Roman, Reynon, 16 |65|.
Roof, Rudey, 20 |25|.
Rook, Thos. James, 16 |42|.
Rose, Jonathan, 18 |68|.
Ross, David, 11 |15|, 13 |19|, 27; John 11 |205|.
Rouff, Rough, Anthony 19 |67|; Geo. 16 |16|; John, 17 |74|; Mathias, 19 |75|; Michael, 19 |66|; Nicholas, 17 |112|; Peter, 16 |17|.
Roughside, Wm. 9 |76|.
Rozer (Roser), Henry, 29 (2), 30, 31 (2), 32 (2), 33, 34, 35 (3), 36 (2).
Rue, Isaac, 19 |61|.
Ruglass, James, 3 |43|.
Runkle, Jacob, 23.
Russell, Callob. 16 |128|; Henry, 5 |419|.
Rutter, Abraham, 15 |13|; Alexander, 18 |108|; Conrad, 15 |15|; Edmond. 18 |110|; Edward, 18 |106|; John 18 |107|; Thomas, 15 |42|; Wm. 18 |109|.
Rynagen, Rynagon, Rynegar. George, 4 |378|; Henry, 4 |392|; Joseph, 4 |380|.
Ryon, John of Wm., 34.

**S**

Safety, Council of VII. 29.
Saffel, Chas. 2 |45|; Wm. 2 |29|.
Sage, Thomas, 23.
Sailler, Sailor, John, 20 |249|; Mathias, 21 |55|; Peter, 20 |247|.
Sallerday, Frederick, 14 |153|; John, 14 |154|; Philip, 14 |161|.
Salmon, Christopher, 15 |56|; Danl. 15 |59|.
Salter, Saml. 19 |137|.
Sam. Nicholas, 13 |61|.
Samto, Thomas. 11 |40|.
Sanders, Chas. 9 |63|.
Sandman, Jacob, 18 |86|.
Sands, Thomas, 18 |72|.
Sansbury, Isaac. 26, 27. 28, 32, 35 (2): Thos. 5 |60|; Wm. 2 |109|.
Savage, John, 21 |54|.
Scears, John Jr., 37.
Sceittner, Martin, 19 |120|.

Schloser, Henry, 13 |27|.
Schnebely, Henry, 19, 20; Henry Jr., 19, |198|; John, 20 |265|.
Schnegenberger, Christian, 19 |23|.
Schnell, Henry, 20 |248|.
Schnertzell, Geo., 24.
Scott, Geo. & Saml. 23; Wm. 37 (2).
Schuhman, John, 19 |115|.
Schultz, Geo. 19 |111|, 20; Jacob, 15 |33|.
Schweitzer, John, 19 |191|.
Schwengel, Geo. Jr. 19 |167|; Nicholas, 19 |162|.
Scibert, Jacob 17 |35|.
Scissell, John, 28; Thos. 31, 33.
Scofield, John, 14 |96|.
Scott, Chas. 9 |4|; David, 21 |91|; James 14 |172|; John, 16 |122|, 21 |90|; Richd. Keen, 26; Thos. 7 |43|; Wm. 21 |92|.
Scrivener, Scrivenor, Richd. 37 (2).
Seaborn, John, 10 |35|.
Seager, John, 2 |12|.
Sears, James, 9 |36|, |102|; Wm. 9 |34|.
Secttner, John Conrad, 20 |212|.
Sedwick, John 8 |84|; Wm. 8 |89|.
Seigeart, John, 17 |104|.
Sehhfeet, Geo. 23.
Seitzler. Wm. 19 |33|.
Selby, John, 28; John Smith, 31, 35; Joseph, 26, 28; Richd. 2 |110|: Saml. 3 |9|; 11 |43|; Thos. 2 |82|: |104|; Wm. 13 |33|; Wm. Wilson, 26; Zachariah, 2 |108|.
Selhart. Godfrey, 20 |16|.
Seller. Jacob. 19 |190|.
Sellings. "Hichard," 3 |185|.
Sellman. Babar, 23.
Semms, Ignatus. 14 |90|.
Sergeant, Elisha & James, Sr. 23.
Serlott, Nicholas, 13 |1|.
Seybert, Geo. 2 |44|.
Shaffer, Conrad, 24.
Shailer, Shaler, Shaleer, Geo. 24; Michael, 18 |141|; Peter, 18 |142|. 24.
Shally, Peter, 13 |12|.
Shank, Peter, 18 |138|, |140|.
Shanton, Ramon, 14 |34|.
Sharer. Geo. 18 |113|; Isaac, 18 |114|; Jacob, 18 |115|; Peter, 18 |121|.
Sharlock, James 8 |123|.
Sharpsburg Hundred. 13.
Shasto, James, 4 |333|.
Shaver. Adam, 23; Geo. 17 |102|; John, 18 |135|: Peter 17 |116|; Powell, 17 |103|.

Sunon, Peter, 21 |93|.
Super, Christr. 24.
Suter, James 6 |131|; John, 2 |55|.
Sutherland, Alexander, 7 |48|.
Swails, Wm. 18 |73|.
Swain, Swan, Swann, Edward 25, 32; Geo. 16 |88|; James, 36; Robert, 3 |195|; Zephoneah, 11 |208|.
Swank, David, 15 |26|; Jacob, 18 |117|; John, 18 |118|.
Swaringen, Swearingen, etc. Chas. 18 |112|; Saml. 3 |148|, 14 |113|; Thos. 5 |110|, 4 |252|; Van 8 |23|, 14 |139|, 15 |29|.
Sweny, Owen, 6 |125|.
Swinchet, Job, 24.
Swingly, Geo. 18 |124|, |126|; Leonard, 18 |144|; Michael, 18 |125|; Nicholas, 18 |134|.
Sylaser, Michael, 13 |22|.
Symmer, Alex. 25 (2).
Syster, Daniel. 18 |127|; Michael 18 |128|.

**T.**

Talbard, Thomas, 16 |118|.
Talbott, Talburtt, etc. Basil, 11 |179|; John, 9 |80|, 27, 29; Notley, 11 |186|; R:chd. 24; Thos. 10 |64|; Wm. 8 |3|.
Tamin, Ambroce, 13 |14|.
Tannehill, Tannihill, Jas. 28, 31, 33; John, 3 |151|; Ninian, 7 |8|; Wm. 4 |315|.
Tarwalter, Jacob, 15 |31|.
Taul, Arthur Thomas, 10 |144|.
Tax Commissioners, 1777, 21.
Taxables, male, 12, 22.
Taylor, James 2 |101|; John, 9 |60|, 17 |114|; Wa'ter, 8 |72|; Wm. 29, 30 (2), 35.
Teachler, John, 20 |24|.
Teeple, Isaac, 2 |53|.
Tennerly. Wm. 33.
Tesern, Frederick, 17 |33|.
Test Book, Montgomery Co. 1780, 11.
Teter, Jacob, 13 |14|.
Their, Michael. 19 |68|.
Thomas, Gabriel, 24; Jacob, 19 |157|; John. 24; John Allen. 32 (2). 34. 35. 36; Martin, 9 |79|: Richard, Jr. 5 |476|; Robert. 7 |3|; Saml. 3d. 5 |467|; Wm. 11 |199|.
Thomer, Ludwig. 19 |2n9|.
Thompson, Thomson. Tompson, John 6 |54|. 12 |41|; John Baptist, 10 |76|: John Dockery, 22; Joseph. 17 |118|; Richd. 8. 9, 11 |5|. 11 |50|; Wm. 6 |64|, 9 |53|, 14 |110|; Zach, 6 |118|.
Thornin, Alworth. 16 |72|.

Threlkeld, Therkeld, etc. Henry, 8 |39|; John, 8 |10|; 11 |39|; Joseph 6 |59|.
Thresher, John, 24.
Tilghman, Edward, Plate IV.
Tilley, Tilly, John, 27, 28; Thos. 32.
Tippery, Jacob, 24.
Tole, Stephen, 5 |109|.
Tomlinson, Tomblinson, Benj. 15 |41|; Hugh, 11 |166|; Humphrey B. 10 |42|; John, 15 |13|; Wm. 10 |126|.
Tomson—see Thompson.
Topping, James, 7 |77|.
Townshend, Leonard, 36.
Tracy, Alexander, 6 |17|, |68|; Philip, 7 |7|; Timothy, 16 |50|; Wm. 2 |20|, 8 |52|.
Trail, Archibald, 2 |123|; Basil, 2 |27|; David, 2 |24|, 47; James, 2 |83|, 5 |451|; Wm. 2 |88|.
Tramell, Philip, 16 |107|.
Trapp, Christian, 19 |49|.
Tresal, Goodhart, 20 |31|.
Trissler, Jacob, 9 |96|.
Troseel, George 15 |7|.
Trott, Trout, Edmund. 7 |53|; Henry, 2 |100|; Mike, 24; Saml. 37; Saml. of Thos. 37.
Trotter, Loudon, 15 |40|.
Troxal, Abraham 19 |84|, 20 |32|.
Trueman, Thos. 26, 27.
Trumpower, Leonard, 17 |98|.
Trundel, John, 7 |62|: Josiah, 7 |95|; Thomas, 4 |321|.
Tucker, David, 3 |111|; Jacob, 7 |34|; John, 3 |110|, 6 |34| Jno. of Edwd. 6 |65|; Jonathan, 6 |81|; Joseph, 4 |359|: Thos. 4, |332|; Wm. 8 |130|.
Turner, Alexander, 37; Chas. 24; James, 13 |18|; Kirkwood, 37; Philip, 27, 29; Saml. 8 |2|; Shadrack, 34; Wm. 37.
Turnbull, John, 34.
Tussy, Jacob, 13 |71|.
Tutw:ler, Henry, 20 |31|.
Tyler, Robert, 32; Saml. 29, 31, 32.
Tvscr, James, 24.
Tysher, Peter, 21 |104|.

**U.**

Uhrenban, Jacob, 19 |36|.
Ultheart. Lawrence. 21 |66|.
Unsell, John, 20 |34|.
Upton, George, 33.

**V.**

Valentine. Frederick, 15 |40|.
Vanswearingen—see Swaringen, etc.
Veals. Daniel. 10 |139|.
Veatch, Hezekiah, 10 |55|;

John 11 |191|; Nathan, 10 |49|; Ninean, 11' |176|, |197|; Richd. 9 |35|; Thos. 10 |151|.
Venebils, John, 4 |368|.
V:ers, Elijah, 10 |110|; Wm. 10 |109|.
Viley, George, 7 |52|.
Vincent, Benjamin, 4 |381|.

**W.**

Wade, John, 13 |14|.
Waggoner, Wagoner, Francis, 20 |9|; John, 19 |93|; M!ke, Jr. 24; Peter, 18 |160|; Phillip, 13 |26|.
Wailes, Benjamin, 28.
Walch, William, 18 |80|.
Walford, Adam, 21 |74|.
Walker, Isaac, Jr. 28; John, 18 |149|; Robert, 10 |48|; Wm. 10 |20|, 13 |3|.
Wallace, Wallise, Alexander, 4 |367|; Harburt, 8 |132|; James 8 |94|, 9 |65|; Nathl. 8 |95|; Wm. 8 |101|, |115|, 10 |152|, 11 |1|; Zephaniah, 8 |32|.
Walling, Delashmut, 20 |2|; James 12 |1|, 20 |1|.
Walls, Hathan (Nathan?) 18 |81|.
Walter, Clement, 6 |77|; David, 11 |194|; Geo. 9 |30|; Jacob, 14 |25|; Wm. 13 |13|.
Walters, David, 4 |312|; Josephus, 4 |275|; Levy. 9 |31|; Thomas, 5 |474|; Weavour, 3 |142|; Wm. 4 |244|.
Warble, Philis, 24.
Ward. Benj. (of Joseph), 6 |22|; Cosnealve, 16 |43|; Edwd. 15 |69|, 16 |140|; Henry. 14 |69|: Jacob, 17 |88|; John. 8 |106|, 22; Joseph, 5 |475|; Richd. 37.
Ware, Martin. 21 |69|.
Warger, Richd. 6 |152|.
Waring, Basil. Jr. 30; James, 32. 33. 34; James Haddock. 28; John, 30 (2), 32 (2), 35.
Warkin, Peter, 12 |17|.
Warman, Warmans, Stephen, 10 |83|, |98|.
Warmer, Saml. Snr. 9 |8|.
Warner, Peter Sr. & Jr. 24.
Warren, George 10 |75|, |131|; John 10 |133|; Thos. 9 |13|, 10 |130|.
Warring. Thomas. 15 |5|.
Washington Co. Md. 12-21.
Waskey, Augustus, 24.
Waters, Geo. 13 |28|; Isaac 2 |16|; James. 6 |53|; Joseph, 14 |128|; Nancy, 2 |17|; Richd. 4 |314|; Wm. 2 |79|, 35; Zachariah, 2 |78|.
Watk:ns, John. Jr. 6 |41|; Leonard, 9 |32|; Thos. 22.

Yost, Henry, 18 |161|; John, 9 |101|; John, H. D. 24; Lodowick, 2 |140|; Tobias, 2 |64|.

Young, Abraham, 8 |111|, 34; Casper, 24; Eustachius, 19 |124|; Geo. 19 |69|, |77|, 22;

Jacob, 22; James, 24; John, 4 |325|, 10 |47|, 19 |208|, 24 (3); Ludwig, 19 |13|; Michael, 15 |8|; Notley, 26, 27; Peter, 8 |96|, 24; Philemon, 37; Saml. 15 |44|.

Z.

Zachariah, Jacob, 18 |163|.
Zacharias, Danl. 24.
Zapp, Geo. 20 |267|.
Zimmerman—see Simerman.
Zott, Michael, 19 |3|.